# PRAISE FOR
# WHOLEHEARTED FAITH

"A touching series of essays in which Held Evans, with Chu's invisible pen, explores how one might find a path forward in Christianity beyond conservative evangelicalism."

—*The New Yorker*

"What readers will find in these pages—what I found—was someone deeply human: funny, irreverent, curious, wise, forgiving, nonjudgmental. She admits that a person of faith has doubts, carries anger, and sometimes cannot reconcile, or carte blanche accept, certain aspects of Christianity. She shows us ourselves."

—*The Washington Post*

"Tackles topics like grace, doubt, and sacrifice while somehow embodying the advice of its first author to its second: 'Thick skin, tender heart.'"

—*New York Times*

"I love everything Rachel Held Evans wrote, and I love her profound, warmhearted, brilliant storytelling. Her books have always thrown the theological lights on for me, charmed the pants off me, entertained and enlightened me."

—Anne Lamott, author of *Dusk, Night, Dawn*
and *Help, Thanks, Wow*

"A voice like Rachel's endures in the time machine of her writing. All who love the sound of it owe Jeff Chu a deep bow. A vision like hers outlives a single lifetime. What she discovered, she made available to us; now it's our turn to carry on."

—Barbara Brown Taylor, author of *An Altar in the World* and *Learning to Walk in the Dark*

"Like all of her work, [*Wholehearted Faith*] is warm, wise, and intimate. . . . Evans doesn't shame the ignorant. She delights us into knowledge on the way to wisdom. . . . One can see why Evans's critics pounce. She likes to draw out their poison to bring healing."

—*The Christian Century*

"A lifeline for disenchanted Christians. We are fortunate to have it as her last word."

—Spirituality & Practice

"Her quest to liberate her faith from fundamentalism garnered her a wide following of devoted fans. . . . Evans's honest questioning of Christian teachings and a God she mostly (but doesn't always) believe in will strike a chord with believers and agnostics alike."

—*Library Journal*

# WHOLEHEARTED
# FAITH

## ALSO BY RACHEL HELD EVANS

*Inspired:*
*Slaying Giants, Walking on Water, and*
*Loving the Bible Again*

*Searching for Sunday:*
*Loving, Leaving, and Finding the Church*

*A Year of Biblical Womanhood:*
*How a Liberated Woman Found Herself Sitting*
*on Her Roof, Covering Her Head, and*
*Calling Her Husband "Master"*

*Faith Unraveled:*
*How a Girl Who Knew All the Answers*
*Learned to Ask Questions*

*What Is God Like?*
with Matthew Paul Turner
illustrated by Ying Hui Tan

# WHOLEHEARTED FAITH

# RACHEL HELD EVANS

*with Jeff Chu*

HarperOne

*An Imprint of HarperCollinsPublishers*

HarperCollins books may be purchased for educational, business, or sales promotional use. For information, please email the Special Markets Department at SPsales@harpercollins.com.

FIRST HARPERCOLLINS PAPERBACK PUBLISHED IN 2022

*Designed by SBI Book Arts, LLC*

Library of Congress Cataloging-in-Publication Data is available upon request.

ISBN 978-0-06-289448-9

22 23 24 25 26   LSC   10 9 8 7 6 5 4 3 2 1

*For Henry and Harper—*
*May you live and love wholeheartedly,*
*no matter where the journey of faith takes you.*

*For Kathleen Gleason*

*For Jill Noga*

# CONTENTS

# CONTENTS

# FOREWORD

I remember Rachel's tone that day more than her words. Something was wrong. She called me into her office to take a look at her laptop. After restarting, the word processor reopened all documents previously active before that damned silver glowing clam decided to update itself and restart. But the words she expected weren't there. Thousands of carefully selected, painfully organized, dutifully placed words. Gone. She'd completed about 20 percent of a new book. The first book of her biggest contract yet. And now it appeared that most of it was lost to the binary grave of technology.

*Okay, breathe. This shouldn't be a problem.* As Rachel's tech consultant, a hat often worn atop my husband cap, I had robust autosave and backup procedures in place. We'd learned our lesson ever since the dreaded Chai Tea Latte incident, a moment from our past we'd come to remember simply by a redundant pronunciation of the drink's name. That one left us with our first few gray hairs and a story that could best be enjoyed through the eyes of others once we'd had some time as an emotional buffer.

However, as with most technical things, my backup system worked only if it worked and for some reason it hadn't. File search? Nothing. Latest backed up file? At least a month old.

Rachel's urge to vomit led her away from the vicinity. Fortunately, Google still worked. After a few desperate searches, a glimmering flicker of hope ignited a wildfire of motivation. I learned there was a hidden folder that contained temporary autosaved files that wouldn't show up in a file search. I called Rachel back, and with a few clicks, we'd done it. Found all eleven thousand words of her next book that minutes ago we'd thought were gone forever. Just in time, too, because our baby was hungry and our three-year-old was up from his nap.

A month later Rachel got sick and never recovered. She died May 4, 2019. The eleven thousand words we found that day are part of this book you hold in your hand. This manuscript isn't what Rachel originally envisioned. Our life today isn't what she envisioned. Being dead at thirty-seven isn't what she envisioned. But that's the thing about having vision. It's not about always being right about the future. It's about constantly learning what's right and striving for it. And that's the vision Rachel had. It's a vision of uplifting people and ideas that benefit the marginalized. It's a vision that lives on. Her stubborn hope for a better future was all-encompassing. She lived more life in her short time with us than most people twice her age. She prioritized doing well at what's important, and she discarded her imperfections with the chaff of each day.

While I might fret over a sopping wet sponge left in the sink, Rachel would be lost in thought considering how to best use her growing influence to come alongside those relegated to the margins. While I ensured every penny spent on expenses was properly entered in our bookkeeping software, she would track down talks and read articles written by talented people not yet in the spotlight. While I wrote code for websites that would need updating in a year, she wrote words to exist for lifetimes.

Jeff Chu rode with me from the hospital back to our accommodations the night Rachel died. Jeff was there in the morning as we decided how, exactly, to let the world know what it had lost. In the coming days and weeks, the *New York Times* ran an obituary. Hillary Clinton tweeted condolences. Jeff traveled from New Jersey to Tennessee to cook me food. In addition to his culinary skills, he is an accomplished writer. He has written extensively for national publications, is a ruthless editor and a dear friend. After Rachel's death, I asked him to take some of her unpublished work, unrealized ideas, and start sewing together a new manuscript. Without hesitation, the instant I had enough jumbled words out of my mouth for him to comprehend my request, he'd already said yes. Like so many friends during this time, Jeff showed up.

In this work you will find Rachel's voice, but more than that, I hope you see her vision. May you understand the best way to remember Rachel is to embody her approach to others, her approach to faith and doubt, her approach to this fragile, fleeting life. Wholehearted.

—Daniel Jonce Evans

# YOU DON'T READ THE
# INTRODUCTION?

*Dear Rachel,*

*I remember the horror on your face when I revealed this previously unknown part of myself to you. Your expression was equal parts disbelief and realization. This is who you married. The spark in your eyes told me you already had a playfully poignant tone prepared for situations like this. Your words followed that spark like a warm, correcting blaze. "You don't read the introduction?" "Not usually, no, I . . ." Realizing, perhaps, this may be the end of our young marriage due to a gross oversight, I started fumbling with cadence to find the one that could best fit the now obvious bad news I was delivering. "I typically start with chapter 1." "Sweetie! Oh my gosh!"*

*As you explained the significance of my error, I decided that since this was so important to you, there was only one thing for me to do: double down. "I just feel like the important stuff will be included in the actual book." To me, the escalating banter that ensued, as we sparred without injury, became more valuable than either of our opposing arguments. But I won't speak for you. I imagine it was your grace alone that allowed our relationship to continue past that hurdle.*

*I read the introduction to this book,* Wholehearted Faith, *and couldn't get through it without tears. If I hadn't learned to reconsider vulnerability as strength (thanks, Brené), I would have counted my tears as a polemic bolstering my case. Jeff has done a wonderful job here; he has taken your words, tone, and spirit, and completed your work. I wish you could see it. I wish you could read it.*

*You talked about the risk of yes; I am left here to share the consequences of it. We said yes. You and I said yes to risk, yes to life together until death, yes to kids. You and I said yes to the unknown, unforeseen consequences of commitment. I once thought "Till death do you part" meant separation when a partner dies. I realize now some commitments last until we're both in the grave. There are parts of you that I strive to carry on. Or perhaps, they carry me. I want them to live for our children, for our friends, for the readers whose lives you changed. I am thankful for the parts of you that balance the weak parts of me. And even if I don't always find the strength to adequately continue the best parts of you in this world, I wish you could know that now, when I pick up a new book, I read the introduction.*

*Love,*
*Dan*

# INTRODUCTION

"How can I help?"

That's how I first encountered Rachel Held Evans.

A few months before my book came out, my publisher received an email from her. She was already ascending from Christian-blogger famous to Christian famous. I was a full-time journalist in New York City. After some years away from the church, I had recently, hesitantly joined one. I didn't read Christian blogs—or any blogs, really. I hadn't heard of her books. I had no idea who she was. But a friend told me that Rachel had been on *The View* and that she was a Big Deal.

"How can I help?"

Who would say that to a total stranger?

Rachel would.

She ended up inviting me to guest-post on her blog, and in the subsequent years, she popped into my life again and again, by email or by text—always encouraging, always offering a snarky observation, always speaking a word of hope. We began meeting up whenever we were attending the same conference or event. When I was traveling through Tennessee, she and Dan welcomed me into their home and drove me through the gorgeous countryside, where we stopped at a farm to buy some apples. "Agritourism!" Rachel said. With her quirky humor and the love emanating from her enormous heart, she bossed her way into my life and stayed there.

In 2015, when she and Nadia Bolz-Weber started a conference called Why Christian? she invited me to do a breakout session—and then the following year she asked me to tell my story on the main stage. I am not a natural speaker; my legs still tremble each time I'm at a lectern or in a pulpit. I'd much rather be sharing with you as I am now, in writing. But Rachel, one of the most stubborn people in my life, cajoled my instinctive no into a reluctant yes. When she and Sarah Bessey launched Evolving Faith in 2018, she did it again, and a few months after that inaugural conference, she called and asked if I would become a partner in that gathering.

The trajectory of our relationship is not unique. I am just one of an enormous—and enormously diverse—group of people who can testify to Rachel's generosity with her time, her energy, her contacts, her platform. She had a particular desire to boost those of us who had typically found ourselves on the outskirts of the church, whether it was because of racism, homophobia, misogyny, ableism, transphobia, or some other unjust bias against an aspect of our identity. If someone tried to silence us or tell us to settle down, Rachel would use every resource at her disposal to amplify our voices and to give us a way to rise up.

Rachel was so many things: One of my best teachers. One of my favorite correspondents. One of my examples as a writer. One of my models as a voice that was both pastoral and prophetic. One of my most faithful advocates. One of the world's most relentless embodiments of Christlike love and wicked humor. But above all, she was my friend—a person who dispensed wise advice and listened so well and dried my tears and teased me fearlessly and texted me while she was breastfeeding to let me know that I was on her mind and that she hoped this wasn't some weird situation in which the Holy Spirit was telling her that I might be dead.

I lost count of the number of times Rachel reminded me: "Thick skin, tender heart." She meant that I needed to learn to let baseless critiques roll off me—"There will always be critics," she said—as I took the risk of opening myself to goodness and love. I would sometimes respond half jokingly that I was actually pretty good at the tender heart part, especially if by "tender" you mean "prickly" or "oversensitive" or "hypercritical." (Even as I type these words, I can hear Rachel admonishing me: "Jeff Chu!") But another part of my hesitation was that opening yourself up to goodness and love also exposes you to the possibility of loss and pain.

Early one morning in May 2019, I was at a coffee shop in Princeton, scrambling to finish the last papers of my final semester of seminary. My cell phone started to buzz, and a name flashed on the screen: Dan. Shortly after Why Christian? Rachel had fallen ill. She was eventually placed into an induced coma in the hopes that her body might heal, and she'd been transferred from their hometown hospital to Vanderbilt University Medical Center in Nashville.

"Hey, Dan," I said tentatively. I tried to steady my voice, but my heart was thumping in my ears.

"Hey, buddy," he said.

The crack in his voice and the silence that followed told me most of what I needed to know.

"If you want to say goodbye, you should get here as soon as you can," he said.

By nightfall, I was at her hospital bedside. Though Dan had tried to cozy up the space with photos and mementos, the room, humming clinically with its life-prolonging machinery, felt as cold as Rachel had been the epitome of warmth. I will not tell you what exactly I whispered into her ear as I held her hand—some things ought to remain between friends. But I will tell you that my tears were tears of both tremendous sorrow and boundless thanksgiving, some of the deepest grief I've ever known mixing with some of the most profound gratitude.

Later that night, a few of us, a motley collection of friends and family, diverse in life experience and theology but united in our love for this beloved child of God, gathered around her. We prayed the Nunc Dimittis, and some of us sang "It Is Well with My Soul." I say some of us because it was not well with my soul, not at all. And I couldn't even pretend enough to sing a single word.

*How can I help?*

Some months after we said goodbye to Rachel, when Dan called to ask if I would finish the book that Rachel had begun, of course I wanted to say no. I'm not Rachel. I am the furthest thing from a straight, white, Southern, evangelical-turned-Episcopalian woman. I am not a parent. I have not read as widely as Rachel. I cannot multitask like she could. I will never tweet with the brave abandon that she did. I'm not sure I can even watch an entire football game anymore, let alone abide the Crimson Tide. Nor can I be for you what Rachel was for so many of us. But I had to say yes, if only because I couldn't bear the thought of possibly seeing her again someday—as Rachel said, "on the days when I believe . . ."—and having her chide me for not stepping up.

Indulge me one more brief memory: The day before her funeral, I went to Rachel's house and descended the stairs to the basement, to her desk. I sat in her chair, but only for a moment, until it felt wrong and even sacrilegious. I stood, and I looked at the corkboard above that desk, where she had pinned encouragements to herself, things that she wanted to remember as she wrote to you and for you. The words that stood out to me most: "Tell the truth."

So let me tell the truth: This is not the book that Rachel would have written. Yet it is still her book, through and through. As you read these pages, I hope you will hear her shining and incomparable voice—wise and witty, curious and courageous, faithful and gracious. I hope you will feel her incomparable presence—her great hope, her warm embrace, her sense of tremendous possibility. And especially if you have been hurt by the church, I hope you will sense her true solidarity.

At the time of her death, Rachel had finished a significant portion of the book, which was tentatively titled *Wholehearted*

*Faith.* The bulk of what you will read in the following pages came from that incomplete manuscript, which I bolstered with my own research. I did my best to follow in her formidable footsteps, tracing the crumbs she left behind. Dan gave me access to her hard drive, too, a repository of fragments and snippets, suggestions and musings, notes on books she had read and imaginings about the God in whom she placed her trust. You might occasionally hear an echo of a familiar story; some of what you'll read in these pages originated in talks Rachel gave, tweets she tweeted, and sermons she preached. All of it is infused with her thought, her theology (we definitely didn't agree on everything!), her heart.

One of the challenges was that Rachel wrote differently depending on the medium. Sharp and pithy in her tweets, she gave herself more space to muse in her talks. And in her books, she was her geekiest, most winsome, and most eloquent self, roaming widely, daring to wax poetic, and drawing from sources both ancient and modern. I suppose this much was true of all her work: She always grounded herself in her own life experience, believing that the truest work was the most personal. Everything was testimony—faithful witness to the God she tried to believe would never leave her or forsake her, holy confession of the One on whom she risked her credibility and staked her claim. So several chapters in this book also draw on her archive of blog posts as well as our correspondence.

Where there were gaps in the storytelling, I asked those closest to her—including her father, Peter; her sister, Amanda; and most of all, her beloved Dan—to help me fill them. To these dear people, I offer my deep gratitude. Where there was space left to be filled with further thought and reflection, I prayed that the Spirit might meet me to do the work for which I felt so ill-equipped, providing sentences and paragraphs when I felt broken beyond words and lacking in wisdom.

As you read these words, I hope you will not just hear but also feel Rachel walking alongside you, probing with her characteristic curiosity and listening for the questions that dog you on your own journey. My wish is that through this book you might experience the Rachel that I did: a faithful friend, a steadfast companion, and a wholehearted sojourner who asked over and over, "How can I help?"

—Jeff Chu

# WHOLEHEARTED
# FAITH

# BECAUSE THEY SAID YES

When you've been married for twelve years, you know exactly what kind of humor your partner will appreciate as she's actively pushing a baby out of her body, and Dan, sensing it would make me feel confident and safe, had the entire delivery room in stitches that night.

I don't remember much of what he said, but I do remember my obstetrician laughing so hard that I worried she might drop the scissors as she passed them to Dan to cut our newborn son's umbilical cord. And I remember being the happiest I've ever been when that little boy's body was placed upon my chest, all startled and slimy and mine.

The days and nights that followed were, as everyone always says, a blur. One can never prepare for the physical and emotional demands of caring for a newborn for the first time, and I was lucky to have a relatively smooth delivery and postpartum experience. Our lives were utterly consumed with nursing, burping, and maintaining the spreadsheet we meticulously updated with details of our baby's diaper contents to report to the pediatrician, because we were completely, unabashedly those parents.

Parenthood demands the best of you, and then some. It demands more from you than you ever knew you had, and it's empowering to rise to that occasion, to learn something new about yourself, including how you can keep going, riding the waves of laughter and tears—your child's as well as your own—on remarkably little sleep.

Eventually, days became days again, and nights, for the most part, nights. (We still get the occasional 3 a.m. wake-up call.) The more mobile our little guy got, the more we saw of his personality: athletic, intrepid, clever, and curious, with a sophisticated sense of humor and a penchant for bluegrass.

I knew I would love this little boy, of course, but I had no idea I would like him this much. And I'm just so glad I said yes to it all.

***

Don't misunderstand: my yes can be complicated. Some days and some nights, I am too tired, too discouraged, and too overwhelmed by all the beauty and all the evil of this world. I am too overcome by the thought that I am willingly subjecting a child to such wonder and such horror, and I don't want to think any more about it.

On those days and nights, my most honest answer to the question "Why are you a Christian?" is just "I don't know.

Why not?" That might seem like a paltry and pale version of "Yes," but it is a yes nonetheless.

For better or for worse, there are seasons when we hold our faith, and then there are seasons when our faith holds us. In those latter instances, I am more thankful than ever for all the saints, past and present, who said yes and whose faith sustains mine. They believe for me when I'm not sure I believe. They hold on to hope for me when I've run out of hope. They are the old lady next to me in the pew and the little kid behind me who recite the entirety of the Apostles' Creed on my behalf on those Sundays when I cannot bring myself to say all those ancient words wholeheartedly—*Is this what I really believe?* They pray for me when the only words I have to say to God are words that I refuse to allow to be printed on this page, because they would make even my most foulmouthed friend blush.

I've come to believe that wholehearted faith isn't just about coming to terms with the heart that beats inside me. It's also about understanding how God has knit together my heart with the hearts of that old lady and that little kid. Wholeheartedness is about seeing and comprehending my place in a bigger family of faith, just as parenthood has transformed my understanding of my role in a biological and social unit. It is about risking hurt and confusion for the sake of the thing that so many of us seek: belonging.

Perhaps it is because I am neck-deep in a season of motherhood and caretaking that I am more aware than ever of the startling and profound reality that I am a Christian not because of anything I've done but because a teenage girl living in occupied Palestine at one of the most dangerous moments in history said yes—yes to God, yes to a wholehearted call she could not possibly understand, yes to vulnerability in the face of societal judgment, yes to the considerable risk of pregnancy and childbirth, yes to clogged milk ducts and spit-up in her hair and hundreds of middle-of-the-night feedings, yes to scary fevers and learning as you go and all the first-century equivalents of bad advice from WebMD, yes to a vision for herself and her little boy of a mission that would bring down rulers and lift up the humble, that would turn away the rich and fill the hungry with good things, that would scatter the proud and gather the lowly, yes to a life that came with no guarantee of her safety or her son's.

I know that Christians are Easter people. We are supposed to favor the story of the resurrection, which reminds us that death is never the end of God's story. Yet I have never found that story even half as compelling as the story of the Incarnation.

It is nearly impossible to believe: God shrinking down to the size of a zygote, implanted in the soft lining of a woman's womb. God growing fingers and toes. God kicking and hiccupping in utero. God inching down the birth canal and entering this world covered in blood, perhaps into the steady, waiting arms of a midwife. God crying out in hunger. God reaching for his mother's breasts. God totally relaxed, eyes closed, his chubby little arms raised over his head in a posture of complete trust. God resting in his mother's lap.

On the days and nights when I believe this story that we call Christianity, I cannot entirely make sense of the storyline: God trusted God's very self, totally and completely and in full bodily form, to the care of a woman. God needed women for survival. Before Jesus fed us with the bread and the wine, the body and the blood, Jesus himself needed to be fed, by a woman. He needed a woman to say: "This is my body, given for you."

God became vulnerable.

I can't help but read the story this way. God was humbled, choosing to put down roots in a particular family at a particular time in a particular place.

This is even more astounding to me, given that Mary herself was part of the community of Nazareth, which was full of ordinary people who held to bad theology, who gossiped too much, who let political disagreements become wedges between them, and who suffered from the first-century version of taking an ancient promise ("For I know the plans I have for you, declares the Lord . . .") out of context and slapping it on every yearbook photo and Instagram post. Because even God was born into a dysfunctional family of faith, and God did not wait around for ideal conditions before showing up.

We don't like to think of God being vulnerable like that, just as we often don't like to think of ourselves being vulnerable like that. We don't like to think about God needing anyone, because what good is God for us mortals, for those of us who know we need others, if God is needy too?

I wonder whether that is a reason why the story and the place and the role of Mary have been whitewashed and sanitized. In the Protestant tradition, Mary has largely been diminished, as if her veneration would somehow take away from Jesus's glory. In the Roman Catholic sector of faith, she is sometimes so esteemed that we lose track of her humanity—and some people go so far as to claim that Mary experienced painless childbirth. With respect to my siblings who believe differently, I'm not so sure that it is necessary or helpful to dehumanize Mary's experience. I don't think it diminishes Mary's value to know that she feared and struggled as the rest of us do. In fact, I think it enhances it.

To understand Mary's humanity and her central role in Jesus's story is to remind ourselves of the true miracle of the Incarnation—and that is the core Christian conviction that God is with us, plain old ordinary us. God is with us in our fears and in our pain, in our morning sickness and in our ear infections, in our refugee crises and in our endurance of Empire, in smelly barns and unimpressive backwater towns, in the labor pains of a new mother and in the cries of a tiny infant. In all these things, God is with us—and God is for us. And through Mary's example, God invites us to take the risk of love—even though it undoubtedly opens us up to the possibility of getting hurt, being scared, and feeling disappointed.

The beauty of the Incarnation is not just that God came to us in human form. Inherent in the Incarnation is that God came to embody relationship, to remind us that love is personal—and interpersonal.

I have come to believe that I am a Christian because of Mary, and because of Mary's midwife, and because of Mary's spiritual ancestors— Rahab and Ruth, Bathsheba and Tamar. I am a Christian because of a sex worker and a refugee, an assault survivor and a woman who pretended to be a sex worker in order to seduce her father-in-law so that she would have some leverage over him in case he tried to kill her.

I am a Christian because of Elizabeth, Mary's cousin, who had herself been subjected to decades of cruel speculation because her reproductive experience did not align with cultural expectations or with society's norms. Elizabeth's unlikely pregnancy developed alongside Mary's, and she accepted her own call from God, to be a comforter and a friend—a reminder that parenting, as with the rest of life, is never meant to be done alone. Though it is unlikely she lived long enough to see her son, John, baptize his cousin, Jesus, Elizabeth managed to raise a kid who offended the religious authorities and also had the life skills to survive in the wilderness on locusts and honey.

I am a Christian because of women who did what they had to do to survive and taught their children to do what they had to do to survive.

I am a Christian because of Hagar, the only person in all of Scripture who had the audacity to give God a new name. Hagar, an enslaved woman who was forcibly impregnated, had every reason to turn her back on God. Yet there in the wilderness, she recognized that God saw her. So she declared God to be *El-roi*; though the Hebrew is somewhat ambiguous, that's often translated as "the One who sees me."[2]

I am a Christian because of Susanna, Joanna, Mary

Magdalene, Mary and Martha of Bethany, and a whole bunch of other Marys that nobody can ever keep straight. When Jesus needed people to help pay for all his travels and to figure out the food and lodging that ministry on the road requires, he turned to women for help. These women didn't just fund Jesus's ministry. Many of them also traveled with him and shared meals with him. They sat under his teaching, and then they shared those stories, sermons, and lessons with their neighbors. They were his patrons, his disciples, and his friends.

I am a Christian because of women who knew a thing or two about what it means to be vulnerable, to suffer, to work within systems that were bent against their flourishing, to endure hierarchies that were designed to forestall their triumph.

I am a Christian because, when things went south and all signs pointed to failure and nearly all the men had abandoned Jesus after his arrest, it was women who stuck around. It was women who stood witness at the foot of the cross, because that is what friends do: they show up. When the ministry had seemingly gone bust, when the crowds had dissipated and disappeared, when the Empire had reared its ugly head and taken the lives of the innocent, these friends stood in solidarity.

I am a Christian because, amid those frantic final hours on that first Good Friday, women loved Jesus. It was traditionally women's work to anoint a dead body with perfumes and spices before burial. But Jesus was crucified on the eve of the Sabbath, when no such work—indeed no work at all—could be done. Imagine these women's sense of incompleteness and their lack of closure. What might they have done on Holy Saturday, as they urged the sun to go down so that the Sabbath would pass?

Did they pray? Did they sit together in silence, eyes weary from crying? Did they rehash the incomprehensible events that had just transpired, reviewing them in agonizing detail?

I am a Christian because of women who, according to Mark's Gospel, said to one another, "Who will roll away the stone for us from the entrance of the tomb?"[3] Amid their grief, they were worried about logistics.

I am a Christian because, as soon as the sun rose on Sunday, they showed up at Jesus's tomb anyway, burial spices in hand.

I am a Christian because of women who showed up.

I am a Christian because of women who said yes.

The Gospel accounts differ on many, many details. But these seeming discrepancies no longer threaten my faith as they once might have. Instead, I see them as refractions of light through a prism—each described by a different witness. That does nothing to diminish the light itself.

The one thing upon which the Gospels agree is that the first witnesses to the resurrection of Jesus were women.[4]

The theological implications of this are significant. For one thing, doubt-filled skeptic that I am sometimes, I am encouraged that they were the first witnesses simply because they were there—because they showed up. Sometimes showing up half-heartedly is all I can muster in my own faith experience, my own burial spices in hand, with no idea how I might move away that stone that sits between myself and Jesus.

I was in my late twenties before I first heard a woman

preach the Gospel from a pulpit. This seems maddening and bizarre to me now, given my understanding that the entire Christian faith hinges on the testimony of women. Some traditions rightly honor Mary Magdalene as the apostle to the apostles. She was the first person to declare, "I have seen the Lord!" and the first to be instructed, along with another Mary, to go and tell the other disciples, "He has been raised from the dead!"[5] When, on Easter Sunday, congregations everywhere proclaim in chorus, "He is risen!" they are echoing that Mary, the first person to preach the full Gospel.

I realize now, though, that I heard the Gospel preached from beyond the pulpit by many other women, including my mother and my grandmother.

My mother is funny and diplomatic and everything a good Southern woman should be. She has always been the life of the party at church potlucks and bridal showers. I remember waiting for what seemed like hours in the hot car in the church parking lot as she finished talking to people after the Sunday service.

Somehow my beautiful social butterfly of a mother produced a highly introverted, very serious daughter who refused to wear makeup or carry a purse, who walked around scratching her eczema and complaining about how her bad skin was the Pauline thorn in her flesh, and who failed to understand that the issue of eternal damnation is not one you should bring up at a church baby shower. Though all that meant I did not fit into the women's scene at our church, which I know must have bothered my mom a little, she never made me feel bad about it. A fourth-generation schoolteacher, she always had a soft spot for the weird kids, and she taught me from a young age that being different does not make you bad.

Whenever I got scared at night, my mother would let me crawl into her bed. Safely ensconced there, I would listen as she gently sang songs to me that testified to her own faith: "It Is Well with My Soul" and "Great Is Thy Faithfulness." Over time, the rich theology of those songs calmed my mind and soothed my heart, and though I would not recognize it until many years later, the voice of God began to sound a little more like a woman's.

My mom missed out on the feminist movement because she was raised an independent, fundamentalist Baptist. Yet she encouraged me to think for myself, to speak out against injustice, and sweetly, with just a little Southern charm for leavening, to dismantle the damn patriarchy (my words, not hers).

My mother might still be a traditional, Southern, evangelical woman, but I am a Christian because of her and because of her yes.

My paternal grandmother was a Lithuanian immigrant named Mary Rose, who, along with her sisters, Rose Mary and Rosemary (I kid you not), grew up in a devout Roman Catholic home.

My grandmother barely survived polio as a child, and so she always walked with a limp, wincing in silent pain whenever she sat down or rose up. Perhaps to help her cope with this ever-present discomfort, she became dependent on alcohol, and remained so for much of my father's childhood.

Mary Rose was stubborn. She once got on the wrong side of nearly her entire neighborhood because she let my dad play in the sprinklers on the front lawn of their Dallas home with some Black boys from across town. Most of the details are lost to history, but I do know that my grandmother was fierce enough that the others in the neighborhood lost that battle, and my grandparents stayed active in civil-rights work even when it was not socially advantageous for them to do so.

The Jesus who rescued my grandmother from her addiction to alcohol happened to be the Jesus of the Protestant and evangelical variety. Upon her conversion, she wrote a twelve-page letter to the pope explaining all her reasons. And it was because of her that my father was reared an evangelical and so was I, receiving my introduction to the Jesus of that beautiful and fraught tradition at Vacation Bible School and on high school youth trips, in *Adventures in Odyssey* and See You at the Pole, through embarrassing Christian music festivals featuring Carman and Audio Adrenaline, and in the language and culture of American evangelicalism, which I have loved and hated and wrestled with for the past thirty years.

Sometimes I am not sure whether I should thank my grandmother or curse her for all this. But I am a Christian because of her and because of her yes.

꧁ ꧂

Though I didn't have the chance to hear a woman preach for the first couple of decades of my life, I was taught by women, including the two Lindas who taught me in Sunday school. There was Miss Linda with the Short Hair and Miss Linda with the Long Hair. I am a Christian because of them.

I am a Christian because of this retired lady at our church

whose name I cannot even now remember. But I do remember that she committed to praying for every high schooler in the church every single day leading up to graduation, modeling for us a way of coming alongside and loving one's neighbors.

I am a Christian because when I had reached the point of complete spiritual burnout, when it seemed as if everything related to church or the Bible or Christianity was one big trigger just waiting to get pulled, I picked up a book with an intriguing title and the picture of a tattooed Lutheran preacher on the cover. It was called *Pastrix*.

That tattooed Lutheran preacher wrote about baptism and communion and the Bible and the cross in ways that I had never experienced anyone discussing them before. In her words and in her incomparable voice, these concepts seemed real and true again—not exactly safe, but real and true. Somehow her storytelling made me believe that, as she put it, "Before we do anything wrong and before we do anything right, God has named and claimed us as God's own."[6]

I am a Christian because Nadia Bolz-Weber was faithful to her call—because Nadia and so many of my other teachers said yes.

⚘ ⚘ ⚘

Humans are fickle, faith can be fragile, and the church—that rambunctious collection of the fickle and the fragile—is a broken and complicated institution. Wholehearted faith means putting yourself at risk of being hurt by that institution and its people.

Yet I have not managed to find a corner of it where grace cannot break through and where there is not enough spiritual oxygen for that grace to grow. If we make ourselves vulnerable to the possibility of hurt, we also open ourselves to the hope of healing, to the hope of being touched by that ridiculous grace.

So often that grace has appeared in and through the bodies and hearts and souls of women. Love still takes the risk of birth, of fellow sojourners who said yes, of women who embraced the hope of good news by declaring, "This is my body, given for you" and "He loves you" and "He is risen!"

Madeleine L'Engle was another one of those women. She taught me through her writing about the real and inevitable danger of saying yes. "If I affirm that the universe was created by a power of love," she wrote, "and that all creation is good, I am not proclaiming safety. Safety was never part of the promise. Creativity, yes; safety, no. All creativity is dangerous."[7]

So many of us understand the profound truth of her claim. "To write a story or paint a picture is to risk failure," she continued. The kind of love she described is a frightening, wondrous form of vulnerability, of daring: "To love someone is to risk that you may not be loved in return, or that the love will die. But love is worth that risk, and so is birth, its fulfillment."[8]

Most days I believe that—and some days I just want to believe. I join in the long, glorious, and sometimes painful chorus, that song sung over the millennia by the hopeful and the brokenhearted, by the downtrodden and the seemingly forsaken, by mothers and teachers, by survivors and activists, by saints and pastors, by disciples and friends.

I say yes because they said yes.

PART ONE

# WHOLEHEARTED FAITH

## 1

# ON THE DAYS WHEN
# I BELIEVE

On the days when I believe, the sun streaks across these East Tennessee hills, showing me that green isn't one color but a million. The infinite deep blue of the sky feels less like an endless void ready to swallow me whole than an open and generous invitation, beckoning all of us who are prone to wander.

On the days when I believe, the raucous laughter of my kids sounds like the prelude to a grander symphony, a promise of unadulterated joy to come.

On the days when I believe, I regard the tulip tree outside my kitchen window and learn from it. Rooted but flexible, it adjusts to the seasons, offering its abundant nectar to bees and butterflies during times of flowering and then seeds and shade to birds and squirrels after that.

On the days when I believe, I feel enfolded in a story so much greater than my own. It's a story that knits together a thousand generations of saints—which is to say, folks like you and me who wrestle with their questions and their doubts, who interrogate the systems and structures of the society around them, who search for a way to make sense of it all, and who wonder whether they belong and whether they're loved. It's a story that makes audacious claims about a man-god named Jesus and calls us into his outstretched arms.

On the days when I believe, a prayer feels as if it's just another beautiful beat in a long-running conversation. Nothing is withheld. Everything finds its place, whether lament or hallelujah. I'm convinced it is all heard, because it's a whisper into the ear of an attentive God who loves me and whom I love.

And then there are the other days.

Some days I don't have words for my own prayers. Fortunately, I can fall back on missives to the divine written long ago and spoken by the hopeful and the hungry. I think, for instance, of one particular old prayer—one of the oldest, in fact. A Bronze Age construction first uttered in the language of a nomadic tribe toiling in the dark, propitious earth of the Fertile Crescent, its words have greeted every sunrise and sunset for more than three thousand years:

Hear, O Israel: The Lord our God, the Lord is one.
Love the Lord your God with all your heart and with
all your soul and with all your strength.[1]

From the moment human beings could speak of the mystery
we call God, we have spoken in terms of total devotion—or at
least the possibility of it.

Heart and mind.

Body and soul.

Love that envelops the entire self.

No holding back.

No fear.

I too memorized these words long ago, promising, as the
Scriptures say, to "impress them on your children," to "talk
about them when you sit at home and when you walk along
the road, when you lie down and when you get up."[2]

The implicit message here is that the life of faith cannot be
lived half-heartedly, and the faith I profess and pass on to my
children requires nothing less than absolute allegiance.

This gets complicated on the days when I'm not sure I believe in God—or at least any version of God like the one I
grew up with. Even the word "allegiance" takes on a bitter
tinge, loaded with cultural freight and political baggage. And
the language of utter devotion is bedeviled by uncertainty and
skepticism.

Sometimes I have gotten a little help from a first-century
Palestinian rabbi who expanded the famous Shema prayer to
include a second biblical instruction. When asked by a biblical
scholar to name the most important command of Scripture,

Jesus, like any good Jew, responded with an embellishment on the Shema, the colloquial title for the prayer, which is taken from its first word, the Hebrew for "hear": "You shall love the Lord your God with all your heart, and with all your soul, and with all your mind." Then he added that a second command is "like it": "You shall love your neighbor as yourself."[3]

Even on those days when I struggle to believe in God, I cannot deny the existence of my neighbor. One of those neighbors, in the most literal sense, is at this moment carefully driving a lawnmower around a political yard sign I find objectionable—a reminder, in ink on coroplast, of all that threatens to divide us. Learning to love Mr. Smith across the street might not quicken my connection to the divine force pulsing through the universe, but I suppose it's a start.

These next few chapters are about loving God and loving your neighbor, even when that doesn't come easy, even when you're not sure. They're about going *all in* when it would be safer to hedge your bets. They're about how any relationship of consequence involves vulnerability and risk, including one's relationship with the divine, and how a God who asks us to love with all our hearts, minds, bodies, and souls does not suddenly demand we suspend the use of those faculties the moment they challenge long-held beliefs or power structures. They're about my own wrestling with the uncertainty that inevitably comes with faith. They're about the wellsprings of my hope.

These chapters are also about loving yourself. Ironically, many of us who grew up believing in all-the-way faith were also told to check important parts of ourselves at the church door. So I write especially for those who feel fractured by the lie that their faith precludes their doubts, their politics, their biology degree, their cultural heritage, their diagnosis, their sexuality, their intellectual integrity, their intuition, their uncertainty, their sadness, their joy.

I'm not the first to make the observation that to love your neighbor as yourself, you obviously have to learn to love yourself. To love oneself is not synonymous with self-obsession or narcissism—or perhaps it's better to say that to love oneself *well* is not those things. To love oneself *well* is to regard one's place in the world with candor and grace, grounded in a humble realization of one's strengths as well as a clear-eyed understanding of one's weaknesses. To love oneself *well* is to be able to distinguish between what one wants and what one needs. To love oneself *well* means not to diminish the beautiful creature that God made nor to cultivate an outsize image of that same person.

To live and to love like this is not easy. If it were easy, if it came naturally, we wouldn't need that prayer. If we had done well at holding on to its claims, we wouldn't need to return to its admonitions—and it probably would have vanished into history. I think it has endured precisely because it is so challenging—so countercultural, so counterintuitive, yet so worthy of remembering.

To live and to love like this points us toward our true selves, which are part of a greater whole. If unholy religion has contributed to our fragmentation, healthy faith can point us toward our restoration. Faith gives people language and stories with which to draw meaning from their experiences, to see their lives as part of a larger narrative of wholeness and healing. At its best, faith teaches us to live *without* certainty and to hope *without* guarantee. "Faith is the assurance of things hoped for," wrote an anonymous biblical author, "the conviction of things not seen."[4] At its best, faith teaches us to take risks.

To live and to love like this is to live and to love in holy danger. Sometimes we can see love as construction material for spiritual cloisters—safe spaces for our hearts, our souls, our egos. In fact, it's the opposite. Love tears down the walls, and it beckons us out into the wildlands of human existence. "Keeping people safe," Ann Patchett writes in her novel *Commonwealth*, "is a story we tell ourselves."[5]

Perhaps the better story to tell ourselves is that the struggle toward love is worth it. It moves us out of the fragmentation that has marked so many of our lives. And it compels us toward the wholeness for which God made us—and that God embodies. God, too, loves wholeheartedly.

What I didn't understand until recently was that we aren't alone in our risk and vulnerability. When God goes *all in* on us and for us, there's risk and vulnerability for God too. Religious folks don't like to think of God as vulnerable. We prefer theology and imagery that depicts God as powerful and in control, a sovereign chess master dispassionately moving pieces across the board. But I don't believe God's vulnerability is some kind of cosmic kryptonite that serves to weaken the divine; rather, it is beauty, it is solidarity, and it is strength.

On our best days, Christians believe God's most significant act of love put God right in the middle of our messy, dangerous world—as a tiny embryo implanted in the uterus of a teenage girl, as a hungry newborn rooting for his mother's breast, as a man who drank at weddings and cried at funerals, as a human being whose heart broke and soared and skipped beats and, one day, stopped. Because true love can never be coerced or controlled, God does all of this without the guarantee of reciprocation. Divine love, like all love, is freely given and freely received. Even if God promises never to walk away, we can—and we have, over and over.

In my previous books, I've written about my own evolution of faith, my wrestling with the church, and my shifts in the understanding of the Bible. You could say that I have had to examine the various fragmented pieces of my religiosity one by one. (Some people might say that they are spiritual but not religious, but I think the evidence of my life shows that I'm still pretty religious, and I'd be a fool to try to argue against that.) Here, I glean from those previous explorations as well as venture onto new fields, because I'm still evolving, still wrestling, still shifting, still examining. What is this abundant life of faith that Jesus invites us into? In the context of the Christian story, what does it mean to be whole?

The pursuit of wholehearted living has enjoyed renewed interest in recent years, but we dare not mistake it for a fad; nor do I want to reduce it to the spiritual equivalent of an Instagram influencer's lifestyle brand. To live and love fully, to embrace human vulnerability rather than exploit it, to try to make sense of our place in this fragile yet beautiful world, to seek to understand our role in proclaiming God's love and justice—this has been the work of generations. It's the quest that creates our greatest works of art and our most profound moments of quiet tenderness. It's the promise that calls us to greet every sunrise and surrender to every sunset. It's the best hope of our oldest prayers, both on the days when I believe as well as on the days when I don't.

# 2

# MY WICKED LITTLE HEART

I am seven. My mother has wrangled the brown mop atop my head into two cascading ponytails, curled with a barrel iron and topped by ribbons of crimson yarn. I wear a tartan smock, white tights, and black Mary Janes—standard church-wear for a good Christian girl in the late '80s. As I approach the microphone at the front of the church sanctuary, the congregation watches me, expectant and pleased. I am one of their stars, the first to answer questions in Sunday school and earn extra stickers for bringing a friend to Vacation Bible School and just a little closer to Jesus. The church ladies will hug me afterward, leaving me standing in a cloud reeking of hair spray and breath mints. They will tell me assuredly that I have a future in the church, perhaps as a Sunday school teacher or—dream big!—a pastor's wife. My future self will recognize much of what they taught me as problematic, but in that moment, when I am small and so new to the world, I feel important and loved, and that counts for something.

Even though it's a children's service, the darkened windows lend an air of severity to the sanctuary. (If you're in church on a Sunday night, you mean business.) My parents sit in the third row, closer than we'd sit on a Sunday morning but still on our regular side. It all seems a bit like a surreal vision, the people and places familiar yet exaggerated, expected yet strange.

I take a deep breath, my mind conjuring the pages of the spiral notebook I'd studied for weeks in preparation for this moment. I can see the words printed on its laminated pages, feel my finger tracing over them again and again.

I wait for the nod from the teacher. Then I crane my neck to reach the microphone, and with my Alabama accent, I declare, with all my heart: "The heart is deceitful above all things and desperately wicked. Who can know it? Jeremiah 17:9."

I intone it all evenly, as children do when reciting something they can't even begin to understand. Then I march back to my seat among the other giggling second-graders, my desperately wicked heart pounding with the giddy deception of relief.

I memorized hundreds of Bible verses between the ages of five and thirteen as part of the AWANA program at my church. AWANA stands for Approved Workmen Are Not Ashamed, a name that still makes me laugh for its suspicious resemblance to an initiative of the Socialist Youth League. It's actually a popular Bible memorization curriculum named in reference to 2 Timothy 2:15: "Do your best to present yourself to God as one approved by him, a worker who has no need to be ashamed, rightly explaining the word of truth."

Presenting myself as one approved became the mission of my life the moment I sat on the edge of my big-girl bed at age five and prayed with my father to ask Jesus into my heart. I wondered, did my heart lose some of its wickedness after Jesus took up residence? Or did my sin still cloud it up, as if I were stuck in a spiritual smoker's lounge?

I did my best to stifle these questions—or at least I tried to work my way out of them. My family and I attended church at least twice a week. My sister and I went to a private Christian school. Dad worked in Christian education, and Mom quit teaching to stay home with us. We listened to contemporary Christian music and read stacks of Christian books. While we associated with non-Christians from the community, those interactions always carried with them the relentless pressure of winning people to the Lord. Every summer I set about evangelizing my East Birmingham neighborhood—the Mormons next door, the Catholics across the street, the gay couple down the road. No one possessed more skill at turning an innocuous conversation about the weather into an important one about Christ's atoning death for our sins, and no one was more infamous for it. When I glided down the street on my second-hand Huffy adorned with streamers, neighbors quickly drew their blinds closed.

What makes my story different from those of so many others who emerged from the same culture and generation—and what kept me from contorting on the inside to fit the impossible demands of religious fundamentalism—is that Peter and Robin Held are stubbornly, unapologetically, and unrelentingly committed to *grace*. My parents made their home a sanctuary of it. As a result, my childhood was a happy one, which is perhaps my most disqualifying experience as a memoirist.

Sure, my parents made mistakes—all parents do, because their hearts are deceitful above all things too, right? But when it came to the most important thing, they nailed it: they convinced me that, no matter what, I was worthy of love.

Somehow that message of God-given worthiness pulsed with a resonance louder and steadier than the noise generated by a community and a culture that often failed to reinforce it. When my teachers, my pastors, my peers, my Christian-apologetics books, and even my beloved, dog-eared, highlighter-scarred Bible partnered to remind me repeatedly that I was hopelessly rotten to my core, deep down in that very core I just couldn't—and didn't—believe it. I rejected that message the way the human body rejects a transplanted organ that, despite everyone's best efforts and science's most sophisticated drugs, just cannot belong.

Early on I sensed a profound disconnect between what I was supposed to believe and what I actually believed. At home, my parents encouraged questions, and when they didn't know the answers, they said so. But in Sunday school, my precocious inquiries met with furrowed brows, cleared throats, and the not-too-subtle suggestion that good Christians don't ask such impertinent things. At home, we talked about a world that was broken and beautiful, just waiting for us to make our mark on it. At my Pentecostal elementary school, I learned that demons hid around every corner, Bill Clinton was the antichrist (I sobbed when I found out that my grandfather had voted for Clinton for president), and the rest of the world lived in "darkness." My church told me a woman's place was in the home; in my home, Dad told me I could be anything I wanted to be. My Christian books said following my heart would only lead me astray; Mom taught me to listen to my gut.

It wasn't that my parents rejected the teachings of conservative evangelicalism (to this day, they hold to many of them); it was that they held those beliefs carefully and tenderly, with compassion and humility. They never seemed to fear living in the tension—between what they knew and what they didn't, between what they believed and what others believed, between their convictions and their questions. For a kid, parental courage is remarkably contagious.

You would think this relative open-mindedness would have put my parents at odds with our Bible-believing, evolution-denying, Republican-voting community, but even the most hardened fundamentalist respected the Helds as wise and decent people. That's the alluring and mystical beauty of grace: people are drawn to it, even when they aren't supposed to be and even when they don't know why.

I processed all this cognitive dissonance by overcompensating. During high school, I rebelled by becoming even more religiously devout than my parents were. When we moved to Tennessee, I transferred to a public high school, which was clearly God's blessing on my proselytizing spirit; this would, I assumed, provide the mission field of my teenage dreams.

Every morning, as I applied my rum raisin lipstick (circa 1994) and styled my Rachel Green haircut (circa 1997), I listened to DC Talk's "Jesus Freak" (circa 1995) to psych myself up for another day of witnessing to classmates. I accessorized for Jesus: my JanSport backpack boasted a strip of red duct tape upon which I had scribbled "GOD IS AWESOME" with a Sharpie, and my left hand sparkled with a purity ring. What some might have seen as extracurricular activities were really my core curriculum: I served as president of the Bible Club, led devotions over the intercom, and organized the See You at the Pole prayer event each year.

None of these activities proved as socially devastating as you might think—or as they might have been elsewhere. We had moved to one of the most religiously conservative towns not just in the state, not just in the South, but in the entire country: Dayton, Tennessee, home of the famous Scopes Monkey Trial of 1925. When we arrived in Dayton, there were some 5,500 people living here—and more than twenty churches, including a Church of God as well as a Church of God of Prophecy. (Was the former a Church of God of Non-Prophecy?) Just about everyone in town already identified as Christian. So while I was desperate to convert someone, there was actually no one to convert.

Still, every morning a steady bass line pounded from my bedroom.

> What will people think when they hear that I'm a
> Jesus freak?
> What will people do when they find that it's true?

I don't really care if they label me a Jesus freak.
There ain't no disguising the truth.[1]

It wasn't really true. Because I did care. I desperately wanted them to label me a Jesus freak. I very much wanted them to hear, find, and see that Jesus Christ was my loud and beating heart.

If I look back and analyze carefully the inspirations of my dreams of Jesus freakery, I'd have to admit that one of its primary sources of spiritual oxygen was the persecution narrative that sits near the heart of American evangelical mythology. You know some of the features of this narrative—heathens waging a war on Christmas, teachers getting arrested for praying in public school, the feds coming after Jesus freaks for political incorrectness. There was a militant edge to the fight-back, and counterfactual as the narrative might clearly be to me now, back then I was ready to put on my personalized, kid-size full armor of God and enlist for battle.

In hindsight, I see that it was my privilege that protected me from the sharpest edges of my own theology. I am white. I am straight. In my younger years, I served as a poster child for the most popular and protected religion in the country, in a town where my brand of the faith happened to dominate. Whether out of fear or devotion or some combination of both, I happily played by every one of the rules. But back then I didn't even know what privilege was, unless you're talking about the privilege of serving as a young and zealous ambassador for Christ.

All the while, many of my classmates lumbered beneath the weight of these socially imposed Christian regulations and their accompanying expectations. They hid their sexuality. They smiled through racist slurs. They minimized their doubts. They kept quiet about their abuse. At my high school in Tennessee, memorizing Bible verses wouldn't get you labeled a weirdo, but being gay might. And if you were a girl, dressing like a stereotypical boy might.

Now I regret that I didn't understand any of this at the time. So convinced God lived in the boxes I'd constructed, I failed to look for God in God's favorite place: the margins. And yet not a person who knew me doubted whether I was *all in*. My faith was the most important thing about me, and in my own imperfect, cringe-worthy way, I loved God with all my heart, soul, mind, and strength. There ain't no disguising the truth.

The thing about being all in is that it's a hard fall when the foundation gives way. And that's exactly what happened next. After high school, I attended a conservative Christian college that was supposed to answer all my lingering questions about Christian doctrine but instead propagated them. Chief among those questions was how a good and loving God—the God whose grace and compassion I associated with my parents— could condemn to hell the majority of human beings who live on this planet, most for the misfortune of being born in the wrong place and at the wrong time. If only evangelical Christians went to heaven, I reasoned, this left out millions, even billions, of people who had never even heard the name Jesus. It left out whole continents and generations of men, women, and children raised in other faiths. It left out Anne Frank.

We read *Anne Frank: The Diary of a Young Girl* in middle school, and Mrs. Kelly told us that Anne and her sister had succumbed to Hitler via typhus. I prayed for weeks afterward that God might somehow work a posthumous miracle and pluck her from the eternal fire in which I was sure she was being unfairly tormented. I couldn't accept that a good, loving, and gracious God would burn Anne Frank forever.

Years later, I asked one of my theology professors how we could consider to be just and fair any faith that gave the Nazis a better shot at salvation than the Jews they murdered. I was told that my worldview had been corrupted by secular humanism, that I'd allowed hypersensitivity and emotionalism—*my feelings*—to creep into my faith. I was "soft" and "weak."

"God's ways are higher than our ways," my professor said as he casually polished his glasses after class, wiping away my questions as easily as he did the greasy smears on the lenses. "We dare not question the Almighty."

I encountered some variation on this response from many of the friends, professors, and pastors I consulted during these tumultuous years. While some engaged my questions with more thoughtfulness and care, most eventually arrived at the same conclusion: The problem wasn't with evangelical Christianity or with their interpretation of Scripture, their churches, or their God. The problem was with me. The problem was my overly sentimental, insufficiently sanctified heart.

The reason I was troubled by violent and patriarchal texts in the Bible, the reason I found the fossil record compelling evidence in support of evolution, the reason I wanted to embrace LGBTQ+ people as they are, the reason I wrestled with and doubted aspects of the Republican Party platform and even voted for Democrats, was because my heart was in rebellion against God. I was, in the words of Proverbs 3:5, leaning on my own understanding.

That desperately wicked heart of mine simply could not be trusted to sort right from wrong, good from evil, divine from depraved. I needed to stop feeling so much. I needed to start thinking more—but not too much. I certainly needed to stop asking so many questions.

In short, I needed to just believe. But what if I couldn't?

The faith that I had once possessed demanded disintegration. Of course I could use my brain—as long as it led me to the correct, predetermined conclusions about science, biblical interpretation, and public policy. Of course I could use my heart—as long as it didn't empathize with the wrong people or end up on the wrong side of complex moral dilemmas. Of course I could use my conscience—until it grew troubled by certain teachings and actions of the church. Of course I could use my body—as long as it remained heterosexual, cisgender, attractive but not too attractive, feminine but not too feminine, modest, appropriately clothed, restrained, demure, uncomplicated, and especially sexually dormant until my wedding night, at which point it would magically transform into a sex carnival for my husband.

In other words, I could be a Christian as long as I loved God with half my heart, half my soul, half my mind, and half my body. (Actually, maybe just a quarter of my body.) I could be a Christian as long as I surrendered to *Zerrissenheit*.

*Zerrissenheit* is a German word that means inner strife, fragmentation, or, as the philosopher William James memorably translated it, "torn-to-pieces-hood." Most of us know a thing or two about *Zerrissenheit*; even if we have no idea how to spell it or pronounce it, we've felt its shattering effect in our own bones. It refers to the sense of fragmentation and disjointedness we experience whenever we operate out of fear and shame.[2]

Religion has torn a lot of people to pieces. Whenever it has embarked on a quest for purity, crusaded for certainty, strived for survival, religion has done so at great cost, asking so many humans to ignore their conscience, to pretend to believe things they don't really believe, to squeeze into ill-fitting gender roles and cultural norms, to snuff out desires and squander talents, to live one way during the week and another on Sunday morning, to sacrifice sons and daughters on the altar of conformity, to feign certainty, to fake happiness, to strive for perfection, to look the other way in the presence of injustice—indeed, to renounce some aspect of their very humanity.

Systems that teach people to disengage, whether emotionally or intellectually, do not produce healthy individuals. Nor do they foster thriving communities. Nor do they even honor the One who created the minds, souls, and bodies that we're constantly trying to tame. As I've written elsewhere, when you can't look to your own God-given conscience to tell you what's right or use your own God-given mind to tell you what's true or trust your own God-given gut to tell you what's dangerous, you lose the capacity to engage the world in a holistic way, and you risk falling prey to those who might manipulate your fragmentation for their own ends.

We cannot and should not selectively numb ourselves. If we get in the habit of checking out when it comes to our faith, we inevitably begin to check out when it comes to our relationships, our health, our work, our play, and our moral and ethical obligations to one another. We end up wandering around as if we were spiritual zombies, half alive and half dead, unthinkingly taking orders from whoever happens to be in charge. I have known parents who, against every noble instinct in their bodies, refuse even to share a meal with their gay kid because a popular evangelical pastor told them their whole family might end up burning in hell together as a consequence. I have known good people who suffer unnecessarily from the full, unmitigated force of their mental illness because they read a book or a Facebook post that said faithful Christians don't take medication or seek the counsel of a trained therapist.

None of this is the life abundant that Jesus promises. This is not health. This is not peace. And this is not wholeness.

My suspicions that there had to be something more to abundant life led me away from evangelical Christianity. My hopes for a better understanding of abundant life walked me into a spiritual no-man's-land, and eventually into the pews of the Episcopal Church. I know that describing it like that makes the path sound as if it were linear. In truth, my so-called spiritual journey still continues to meander, to circle like Rilke's falcon. I no longer believe Anne Frank is in hell, but neither can I say with any certainty what happens to us when we die. My views on justice, sexuality, politics, and race have continued to evolve, but I still get stuck on ethical questions related to sex and abortion, violence and war. I am a Christian, committed to practicing the way of Jesus, but in my heart, I still have so many questions, and I still have so many doubts.

As it turns out, all of this is pretty normal. Most people live with some uncertainty in life, even with—*especially with*—complex religious and moral questions. Indeed, as I began writing about my experiences on my blog and in my books, a whole community of kindred spirits emerged. Many of them felt as lonely in their questioning as I at times have. They expressed through their letters, emails, and social media posts the affirmation that every spiritual wanderer and religious misfit deeply craves—that I was not alone in this.

Maybe I should have realized earlier that I wasn't alone. My openness was something my parents nurtured. Some might conclude that my mom and dad were foolish to give their two daughters so much latitude when it came to faith, to encourage our questions and curiosity as much as they did. But looking back, I'm convinced the freedom they offered and modeled ultimately saved my faith. Had Christianity been presented to me as a zero-sum game requiring uncritical acceptance of everything I learned in Sunday school, I would have kicked the dust off my shoes long ago. But like so many things, faith is best held with an open hand, nurtured by both boundaries and improvisation, tradition and innovation. What a gift my parents gave my sister and me in their blessing of holy exploration.

The "we"/"us" in this equation is essential. My convictions about uncertainty are something I've come to in adulthood. On reflection, though, I realize that my path toward wholeheartedness was mapped out not alone but with my parents' patient companionship and their unconditional love. I suspect that I didn't recognize their solidarity sooner because so many of us have been trained to see similarity of opinion and conformity of thought rather than a shared posture. It seemed as if I had so many more questions than they did, so many more doubts.

Yet even before I could put words to these ideas, my parents created an environment in which wholehearted faith was never at odds with questioning or with uncertainty. Wholeheartedness means that we can be doubtful and still find rest in the tender embrace of a God who isn't threatened by human inconsistency. Wholeheartedness means that we can ask bold questions, knowing that God loves us not just in spite of them but also because of them—and because of the searching, seeking spirits that inspire us to want to know God more deeply. Wholeheartedness means that we can approach the throne of grace in the confidence of the God who made us, the God who redeemed us, and the God who accompanies us.

The emotional and spiritual hardships of this journey have led some armchair analysts to conclude that I was failing to "look, and ask for the ancient paths," thereby not finding rest for my soul (Jeremiah 6:16), or that my lack of perfect peace indicated that my mind was not steadfast (Isaiah 26:3). Proof-texting pundits reminded me, after all, that Jesus had promised his burden was easy, so my discomfort and my unwillingness to settle for what was plain and clear was a clear marker of my faithlessness.

I still can't see how any of this was plain or clear. And if a childhood in evangelicalism gave me anything, it was the ability to proof-text right back. As Paul writes in his first letter to the Corinthian church: "No one comprehends what is truly God's except the Spirit of God."[3] And later in that letter, he adds: "For now we see in a mirror, dimly . . . Now I know only in part . . ."[4] I have never thought that it should be easy to understand God or God's ways. "If I find Him with great ease," wrote Thomas Merton, a Trappist monk and renowned American spiritualist, "perhaps He is not my God. . . . If I find Him wherever I wish, have I found Him?"[5]

Many of my fellow travelers had been ostracized and alienated by their churches. Some had been distanced by their friends. Some had even been disowned by their families merely for the "sin" of asking too many questions. But acknowledging uncertainty doesn't make a person less faithful; it just makes her more honest. Admitting how much we don't know doesn't make a person less faithful; it just makes him more candid—and perhaps even more curious. Anne Lamott has chronicled the meanderings of the heart as well as anyone, and as she famously puts it, "The opposite of faith is not doubt, but certainty."[6]

When I read that, I found it reassuring. If uncertainty is a marker of faith, then I must be pretty darn faithful. There ain't no disguising the truth.

# WHERE STONE
# BECOMES FLESH

E zekiel was an exile. Deported following the Babylonian conquest of Judah early in the sixth century BCE, he found himself far from home when he began receiving visions and prophecies. I have to wonder how much his nostalgia and his homesickness drove him in his quest for understanding why his homeland had lost its independence and why God's blessing seemed to have evaporated.

Much of the Book of Ezekiel makes for difficult reading, with its harsh judgments, its invocations of God's wrath, and its use of grotesque and sexually loaded allegory. The people had walked away from God for something like the gajillionth time, exploiting the poor and resorting to violence and generally making a mess of things. But Ezekiel is also a book about restoration, redemption, and re-creation. In chapter 36, God makes a promise to the people through Ezekiel: "A new heart I will give you, and a new spirit I will put within you; and I will remove from your body the heart of stone and give you a heart of flesh."[1]

The ancient rabbis understood the Hebrew phrase *lev basar*, which is translated as "heart of flesh," to be a heart that is aware and attentive, to its Creator and to the rest of creation. In an interview with the writer Parker Palmer, Rabbi Ariel Burger explained that he had chosen Ezekiel 36:16 as his mantra for the year and then cited the centrality of *lev basar* in the thinking of an important Hasidic teacher. "There's a Hasidic teaching, from Rebbe Nachman of Breslov: 'There's nothing as whole as a broken heart,'" Burger explained. "In these traditions, you cultivate a broken heart[,] which is very different from depression or sadness. It's the kind of vulnerability, openness, and acute sensitivity to your own suffering and the suffering of others that becomes an opportunity for connection."[2]

Could there be a more beautiful hope or a more lovely promise from God than that of a heart of flesh, a heart of vulnerability?

To recognize God's grace in the provision of a heart of flesh is key. Much as I prefer the self-protection offered by cynicism, caution, and carbohydrates, finding my way back to my own belovedness has required receiving a new spirit, one of tenderness and one of vulnerability. Over the course of the last decade, we have witnessed something of a cultural awakening around the importance of embracing vulnerability in the quest for meaning and connection. The groundbreaking writing of Brené Brown has inspired millions to pursue what Brown calls "wholehearted living," a posture of resilience and compassion that begins with the conviction that "yes, I am imperfect and vulnerable and sometimes afraid, but that doesn't change the truth that I am also brave and worthy of love and belonging."[3] According to Brown, the only way to experience meaningful connection is to stop numbing and start engaging, to lean into uncertainty, risk, and emotional exposure so we can "look at life and the people around us, and say, 'I'm all in.'"[4]

I have kept Brown's books on my nightstand. Her work has been an invaluable force in helping me reintegrate my heart, soul, mind, and body after years of torn-to-pieces-hood. However, in conversations with other Christians, I have found that many are afraid to apply these transformative principles to their faith, for, as Brown herself notes, religion often attempts to make what's uncertain certain. As a result, a good number of my friends and readers hold two seemingly contradictory worldviews. On the one hand, they know that all the happiest, healthiest people are grounded by an indelible sense of worth; on the other, they believe Christian doctrine teaches that their sin makes them unworthy of God's love. On the one hand, they see that honesty and emotional transparency are far better than secrets, lies, or numbness when it comes to nurturing human relationships; on the other, they've been taught that when they approach God, they need to suck in their fears, doubts, anger, and sadness, holding all these things in like a beauty queen squeezing into a ball gown. While experience shows that vulnerability is inevitable, better embraced than resisted, believers often expect that in a world of danger and uncertainty, their faith ought to function as the one certain, invulnerable thing, immune to disappointment, doubt, and change.

But invulnerability is not what we find in the biblical witness or in the testimony of saints past and present. For every psalm of praise, the Bible also gives us psalms of frustration and lament in which the faithful cry out, "Why, O Lord, do you stand far off? Why do you hide yourself in times of trouble?"[5] For every catchy truism offered in Proverbs, we encounter more complicated reflections, like those of the wealthy sage who observed in the Book of Ecclesiastes that "all is vanity and a chasing after wind."[6]

Over and over, we see our ancestors in the faith not only expressing their heartfelt emotions but also acting on them. Far from being a stoic observer of the world, Jesus was often said to be moved by compassion, overcome with joy, or awash with grief. He sometimes appeared conflicted about decisions and was even pleasantly surprised by other people's faith. Abraham pleaded with God, Job argued with God, and Hannah bargained with God. The nation of Israel is named for a man who wrestled so intensely with God that the struggle left him with a limp. The earliest monastics wrote of both ecstatic revelations and dark nights of the soul. Even Mother Teresa, a seemingly tireless advocate for the poor, fought mightily with depression and despair—and at times seemed to lose that battle; once, she confessed in a letter to a friend, "I no longer pray."[7]

These are just a few examples from the Jewish and Christian traditions, but other faiths and practices also acknowledge the fact that imperfection, doubt, and vulnerability are inevitable in the human experience, and thus inevitable to the life of faith. As Christian humanist Daniel Taylor writes, "No significant area of life is free from risk. It is a key ingredient in every accomplishment and every relationship. Whenever a decision is required, there is risk. Wherever we must act, there is risk. Wherever people intertwine their lives, there is risk. Should we expect it to be any different in our relationship with transcendence?"[8]

So perhaps wholeheartedness does not mean reductive thinking that clings to the idolatry of sharp contrasts between black and white but rather a recognition and acceptance of the reality of the vast and beautiful landscape of grays. I have come to believe that wholehearted faith, like all wholehearted living, requires taking risks, cultivating vulnerability, and embracing uncertainty—both in our individual lives and in our communal life together. It demands that we admit all that we cannot know, and it encourages us to pursue it nonetheless.

I believe.

Each time I say those words, which begin the Apostles' Creed, I say them wholeheartedly. I did not grow up in a creedal tradition. But in adulthood, I have found comfort in the fact that, for millennia, aspiring believers like me have found solace amidst their struggle by reciting these words together, Sunday after doubt-filled Sunday, century after sin-ridden century, always hoping for redemption and always hoping that the words might be true.

Don't get me wrong: That doesn't mean I always believe every single word. Rather, it means I *want* to believe. I want to believe in the rich and elaborate story the Creed represents. I want to believe there is a good and gracious God who created all the beauty we can see as well as all we can't—and who redeems all things. I want to believe there was once a man who, like all other men, went to the grave but, unlike all other men, triumphed over it and ascended to a place we don't yet know but will someday. I want to believe there is one holy catholic church, bound together across time and space, in marvelous mystery and faithful companionship, by a Spirit who knits together when we only know how to tear apart. I want to believe in a love so lavish that it overwhelms us. I want to believe in a faith that can handle all my questions. I want to believe in a religion that can not only tolerate but also embrace my whole heart.

The theologian Justo Gonzalez, in his short but significant book on the Apostles' Creed, notes that this brief statement of faith is not what any one of us might have written, were we to compose a summary of our beliefs or our faithful aspirations. "I might find it easier to delete the phrase about the virgin birth," he writes. "And I certainly would want to add something about the social responsibility of believers."[9] I imagine we could each write our own version, emphasizing what matters most to us when it comes to expressing the meaning of God, Jesus, and the church in the world as we know it. But idiosyncratic as some might find my faith to be—heretical even!—the point is not to reinforce my opinions. Rather, it is to claim my belonging in a family. As Gonzalez writes, "I am declaring myself part of that countless multitude throughout the centuries who have found their identity in the same gospel and in the same community of believers of which I am now a part—a multitude that includes martyrs, saints, missionaries, and great theologians, but where in the final analysis all are nothing but redeemed sinners, just as I am."[10]

So I say I believe.

I believe not in spite of all my questions but because of them. I believe not in spite of all the theological points that I undoubtedly have gotten wrong—and the ones I've gotten right—but because of them. I believe not in spite of my sins but because of them, just as I am—and just as all those saints and sinners who came before. My own quest for wholehearted faith began, as I mentioned earlier, with the question "How can I love God with my whole heart if my heart is desperately wicked?" This question led to even bigger ones, for instance, "How can I love God with my whole heart if I'm not even sure God is real?"

Your search might have begun with something else, and your journey might eventually lead you to places beyond the scope of my explorations. Good. That's as it should be. My hope is that you will hear from me an invitation to stop running away from the questions and ideas that frighten you the most, questions and ideas that may overlap with some of mine but that will inevitably be your own, defined by the shapes and shadows of your own experiences—and of your own God-given heart.

My desire is that you face all your questions, all your conundrums, all your contradictions, boldly. I cannot guarantee you will retain the faith you inherited—I know that mine is not exactly the faith that my parents helped to instill in me—and honestly, a static faith or an unchanging one isn't and shouldn't be my prayer for you, because as we learn and as we grow, faith should evolve. In all candor, I can't promise that you'll hold on to any faith at all. But that's the risk we take when we decide to stop pretending, when we agree to go all in without any guarantee that all will stay the same. And somehow I have to believe—no, I want to believe—that the God of the creeds will meet us, as gentle and constant as the shepherd the ancients spoke of, as imaginative and creative as from the start.

I want to believe in the God who moves mountains. I want to believe in the God who stills the seas. I want to believe in the God who promises to transform hearts of stone into hearts of flesh—and I want to believe that the desires of my heart must count for something.

## 4

# THE LIBERATION OF
# THE KNOW-IT-ALL

The religious culture of my childhood taught me to cultivate a particular form of internal dialogue that I'll call the anguish of the mind. I tend to be cautious. (No comment from anyone who follows me on Twitter.) I am pretty skeptical. And I have a tendency to intellectualize, both internally and externally, as a defense mechanism.

As I've thought about why I do this, I've come to the conclusion that brain-based argument helps protect me from being disappointed—disappointed by my own inconsistencies, disappointed by others' frailties, disappointed even by God. If I can just construct a rational explanation, if I can just arrange things so that they make logical sense, it serves to limit the uncertainty—all that is irrational, all that is illogical, all that seems contradictory or paradoxical—that would otherwise bedevil me.

This is the faith of citadel construction, an endless building project meant to stave off unwanted intruders (doubts, questions, Democrats). Day after day, I continue with the business of building my fortress with my thoughts and my tidy internal logic. I arrange the stones and bricks ever so neatly to repel both any unwelcome invasion by my own shaky feelings as well as the obviously less-thoughtful incursions by those who might disagree with me. Much to the chagrin of my patient husband, I've become perhaps too practiced, too deft, at lobbing tweets like cannonballs from the ramparts of my mind.

What I've realized I'm trying to construct with my arguments is a facade of certainty. Though I may have walked away from many of the tenets of my evangelical childhood, it has been far more difficult to reform—or (to use a term that's perhaps less popular among progressives but really no less relevant) repent of—my fundamentalism. At times it is as if I didn't dismantle that fortress at all. I just took one flag down and raised a different one in its place. That doesn't make the walls any more solid, that doesn't make it any warmer a place to live, and that doesn't make me any more wholehearted a human.

Occasionally people will ask me what I think about absolute truth, which I like to consider an estranged cousin of certainty.

They ask me if I believe in absolute truth and what I think absolute truth is, and sometimes they warn me of my apparent relativism and that proverbial slippery slope. As I've said before, these are complex questions to pose to someone who once lost her contact lens in her eye . . . for two entire days.

It's not that I don't believe absolute truth exists, but if it does, it would take the mind of God to know it in its fullness. I don't think that absolute truth is sitting there in plain sight, waiting to be noticed. If it exists, I imagine it to be more like the wind, gently yet indirectly alerting us to its presence. We might see how it stirs the daffodils into a springtime dance. We might sense how it greets the aerodynamic wings of seagulls, sending them soaring heavenward. We might feel its cooling whisper on our wet skin as we emerge from a swimming pool, or we might understand the life-sapping effects of its withering absence on a brutally hot and humid day. But it's impossible to bottle or to tame.

Occasionally, when I'm reveling in the ancient poetry of the Psalms or a particularly lovely verse of Rilke, I'll imagine that I've stumbled across some nugget of truth. But it's hardly tweetable, as if human language—or at least my limited vocabulary—were incapable of summarizing truth's tremendous sweep in short form. Sometimes I believe I spot its glimmers in other people—in the irrepressible honesty of my kids, in the gorgeous lilt of my singer-songwriter sister Amanda's voice, in the candid company of a few dear friends. But when I try to capture it, well, how do you put the springtime breeze in a box or hold on to the flash of a lightning bug?

Truth might be out there for us to glimpse and even to

explore and to discover, but I don't believe any longer that it can translate into anything resembling certainty. My Twitter feed notwithstanding, I know I don't have an answer for every question. Sometimes I'm not ready to give an answer because I honestly don't know what the best one is—and maybe there isn't even just one best answer. Sometimes I'm not ready to give an answer because I'm finally ready to acknowledge that there's so much I don't know, so when I say that I don't know what the best answer is, what I mean is that I'm not even sure what the options might be.

Saying "I don't know" can be seen as a sign of weakness, as if you haven't spent enough time with your Bible, or as a marker of your lack of conviction, as if the ways of the world were slowly eroding your faith. And in both the Christian and secular worlds, a public admission of not knowing can seem like an irresistible light to the mansplainy moths; did they really think that my candor was an invitation to have my uncertainty addressed by their certainty?

Faith in Jesus has been recast as a position in a debate, not a way of life. But the truth is—heh—I've found people to be much more receptive to the Gospel when they know becoming a Christian and being a Christian don't require becoming a know-it-all. That is a form of faithful freedom too. There is liberation in not having to know everything and not having to impress everyone with that boundless knowledge.

That liberation is rooted in a profound humility, the ability to say that God is God and I am not. Humans have made some enormous mistakes when failing to distinguish between God's perfection and our fallible selves. And many of us have found a renewed sense of possibility when we've realized how much of God's beauty remains to be explored—and that the life of faith is also a life of holy curiosity.

Anyway, most of the openhearted wanderers I've encountered are looking not for a bulletproof belief system but for a community of friends, not for a spiritual encyclopedia that contains every answer but for a gathering of loved ones in which they can ask the hard questions.

I think often of Peter's admonition to "always be ready to make your defense."[1] His exhortation was nestled in a love letter to a persecuted church during the hostile reign of the Roman emperor Nero. He wasn't coaching presidential candidates ahead of a debate; he was counseling potential martyrs. He wasn't offering his readers a course in Christian apologetics; he told them to give "an accounting for the hope that is in you," an embodied profession of the faith that freed them from earthly fear and compelled them toward a steadfast eagerness "to do what is good."[2]

Peter wasn't naïve. He understood that a band of believers modeling goodness in the face of brutality and gentleness in response to cruelty would likely be misunderstood. Yet he also knew that all he could do was equip the faithful to answer the questions they were asked—not only by bellicose others but also by their own fragile, wondering, frightened selves. And he was convinced that the only possible answer was an otherworldly hope in a countercultural love.

Wholehearted, vulnerable faith lives not in the mental citadel but on the open, windswept plains of the heart. And on that vast terrain, we are called first not to proclamation but, once again, to observation, to listening, and to love: "Hear O Israel: the Lord our God, the Lord is one. Love the Lord your God with all your heart and with all your soul and with all your strength."[3]

Peter undoubtedly knew the words of the Shema by heart. I'm sure he needed its reminders too—the instruction to hear, the reiteration that we are summoned to holy attentiveness and to careful contemplation and to faithful witness. He had such a tumultuous life of faith. The record shows that his witness was inconsistent, pockmarked by moments of unbelief. He is the disciple to whom Jesus famously said, after following Jesus onto the waters of the Sea of Galilee, "You of little faith, why did you doubt?"[4] He is the disciple who, three times, denied even knowing his Lord. Yet what little faith he had somehow was enough—*he* was enough—for Jesus to say that, upon that rock, he would build his church.

I wonder whether Peter ever recited the Shema to himself. Did he invoke those ancient words to remind himself of the One who was not only his friend but also his rabbi and his Lord? When, in I Peter, he writes to the faithful that they ought to "maintain constant love for one another, for love covers a multitude of sins,"[5] I have to imagine that he wasn't writing theoretically. Surely he had his own history of sins and shortcomings in mind—his own acts of faithlessness, his own denial of Christ—as well as the memory of the profound love he felt from Jesus.

The words of the Shema would make no sense if the life of

faith were easy. Nor would this prayer even be necessary were we rock-solid and unfailingly steady and sure in our beliefs or our religious practices. It is, like most heartfelt prayer, the exact opposite of an expression of certainty; it's aspirational, an expression of hope and longing.

The Shema was—and is—the mantra of a manna-nourished people, the restorative words of those whose ancestors had wandered the wilderness in search of home. Traditionally, Jews have recited this prayer twice a day, morning and evening; a ritual repetition suggests that we need the regular reminder. Many Jews also have the verses inscribed on miniature scrolls and contained within tefillin, tiny boxes worn during worship, or mezuzot, small cases attached to the doorframes of their homes.

The Shema is, like so many prayers, not so much an act of telling God something about what we are experiencing than a ritual of recentering ourselves—not on our own certainty but on our own faith; not on the futile chase for all knowledge but on the path toward relationship with the only One who can be a true know-it-all; not on ourselves but on the One who made us and the One who is with us. "We are all interconnected in this world, every rock and stone, every creature," says Rabbi Angela Buchdahl, the senior cantor at New York City's Central Synagogue, who grew up reciting this prayer with her sister every night and now does the same with her own three children. The Shema offers a steady reminder: "God is in all things."[6]

But if this were easy to remember, and if this path were painless, and if this journey were easy, and if loving God—or even just recognizing God—weren't so counterintuitive, why exactly would you need all your heart, all your soul, and all your might?

Heart and soul and might: in other words, we are to love God with our whole selves, our whole messy and complicated and conflicted selves. "Those who believe that they believe in God, but without any passion in their heart, without anguish of mind, without uncertainty, without doubt, without an element of despair even in their consolation, believe only in the God-Idea, not in God Himself," wrote the Spanish novelist and intellectual Miguel de Unamuno.[7] In other words, certainty isn't faith. And faith is marked by the humility to let yourself question—which is not a shortcoming but an acknowledgment of one's humanity.

Implicit in that assessment is the conviction that God makes room for our questions and for our humanity, that God is not some legalistic taskmaster but instead the source of grace. The God I have come to believe in is not some stern grandpa in the sky, waiting in quiet exasperation for me to slip up, which I inevitably will, and then tallying up my acts of faithfulness and righteousness versus my deeds of ingratitude or moral failure. The idea of that kind of god doesn't sit well with me at all. Instead, I've come to see God through the things God has done. That God met Peter on the stormy waters of faith and took a holy sledgehammer to my self-constructed certainty. That God is the architect of creation, the engineer of love, and the master artisan who came up with the idea of the heart.

## 5

# THICK SKIN,
# TENDER HEART

In the ancient Near Eastern culture from which the Shema emerged, the heart was thought to be the seat of a person's emotions, the home of the intellect, and the center of the inner life. The Hebrew word for "heart" (*lev* or *levav*) refers not only to impulse and intuition but also to reason and will.[1] The Hebrew vision of the heart, then, is holistic, and wholeheartedness, in the Hebrew context, wasn't just or even primarily about one's feelings. As Amy-Jill Levine writes in *The Jewish Annotated New Testament*, the heart "represents the center of thought and conviction."[2]

Our modern, Western worldview tends to impose a dualism between heart and mind, body and soul, belief and action, and it elevates the rational mind above the fickle heart. "Western philosophy has been worshipping reason and distrusting the passions for thousands of years," Jonathan Haidt writes in *The Righteous Mind*. By way of illustration, Haidt recounts the rough outlines of Timaeus, a creation myth written by Plato, in which a perfect god was populating the world with souls—"and what could be more perfect in a soul than perfect rationality?" The work of creation is, of course, exhausting, so this god decides to let some lesser gods finish the details of creation, among them the outfitting of bodies to go along with the souls. "The deities began by encasing the souls in that most perfect of shapes, the sphere, which explains why our heads are more or less round," Haidt writes. "But they quickly realized that these spherical heads would face difficulties and indignities as they rolled around the uneven surface of the Earth." Thus were human bodies invented, animated by "a second soul—vastly inferior because it was neither rational nor immortal."[3]

This is how Plato imagined the origins of the heart. This is how he explained the human desire for pleasure as well as its response to pain, its propensity for anger as well as its temptations toward lust. This also provided Plato a convenient opportunity to clarify his hierarchy of the genders: Timaeus says that any man "who lived well during his appointed time was to return and dwell in his native star, and there he would have a blessed and congenial existence. But if he failed in attaining this, at second birth, he would pass into a woman."[4] What a curse.

The way we fight, especially in childhood, often contradicts that dualism. Kids somehow innately understand the interconnectedness of heart and mind. You can see it in the way they go for the emotional jugular, whether it's taking the toy they know the other kid wants most or saying the cruel thing that's totally illogical yet completely devastating. As adults, we're not much different, except that the fight often continues with one party trying to claim the alleged high ground by questioning the deployment of emotion. If only the mind were free of the baggage of feelings! If only reason were unencumbered by the troublesome wanderings of the heart!

In spite of its roots in ancient Hebrew thought, the Christianity of my childhood absorbed this duality and this moral hierarchy. Take, for instance, Paul's assertion that the husband is the head of the wife; only with the Greco-Roman elevation of mind above heart does this metaphor have the non-egalitarian power that it has had. (Pop quiz! Q: Where in Scripture does it say, by way of explanation of husbandly headship: "For the male, unless constituted in some respect contrary to nature, is by nature more expert at leading than the female"? A: Nowhere. That's Aristotle, in his *Politics*, but it sounds a lot like Paul, as do the Aristotelian ideas of wives being governed as "free equals" to husbands.) The way so many churches have interpreted those verses deserves to be footnoted with the names of those unacknowledged ancient influencers of Greek and Roman philosophy, whose writings were then calcified through Western practice.

But heart and mind, emotion and thought, enjoy far more integration in the Hebrew Bible. The ancients knew intuitively what the latest research concedes as fact—that we just aren't as rational as we like to think. How we behave affects what we believe, which affects how and what we worship, which affects what we feel, which affects the way we think and rationalize, which affects the stories we tell ourselves and our children, which affects the way we live and love and move our bodies in this world—which is to say how we behave. This process is not linear but cyclical.

Ancient Hebrew thought viewed the heart as an engine of action. It was seen as the muscle that moves us. The "thoughts of the heart" weren't these discrete, contained spiritual thought bubbles but precursors of action. "The logic of Hebrew," author Lois Tverberg writes, "realizes that an action should result from what is in our minds. If you 'remember' someone, you will act on their behalf. If you 'hear' someone, you will obey their words."[5]

Perhaps that's why the eleventh-century rabbi Rashi, revered as one of the great interpreters of the Hebrew scriptures, emphasized that the Shema's instruction is rooted in love. Love is the root of its instruction, and love is the fuel for its action. Rashi taught that humanity's heartfelt obedience had to be motivated by love, not by fear or some other feeling. "The one who acts out of love cannot be compared to the one who acts out of fear," he wrote. "If one serves his master out of fear, when the master sets a great burden upon him, this servant will leave him and go away."[6]

And perhaps that's why the Hebrew word *chesed* appears 248 times in the Hebrew Bible. *Chesed* is a covenantal love, a profound and committed and long-term love, a kind love—

but not a romantic love. Among people, it can take the form of charity; from God to human, *chesed* has qualities of mercy, of grace, and of long-suffering. This kind of love so confounded Miles Coverdale, a sixteenth-century Bible translator in England, that as he worked to translate the Hebrew Scriptures into English, he felt compelled to coin a new word to describe it: loving-kindness. (More recent translations opt for "steadfast love" or simply "kindness." That latter one especially underplays things.)

Here's the point: if we are able to love, as John says, it's only because God has first loved us.

In a YouTube video introducing the Shema, Rabbi Lizzi Heydemann, the dynamic founder and leader of Mishkan, a progressive Jewish community in Chicago, notes that before the Shema is prayed, Jews often recite another prayer call, the Ahava Rabbah (and also the Ahava Olam). Where *chesed* is infused with grace and mercy, *ahava* is all about intimacy, personal connection, and will—and where the Shema calls on the faithful to love the Lord their God, it is *ahava* to which they are being called.

Heydemann translates *ahava rabbah* as: "Big love. Deep love. Abundant, overwhelming sweep-you-off-your-feet, knock-you-over-with-love love. Because that's the kind of love that God had for our ancestors and had for us. But we're so often too busy to even notice. So notice, the prayer says, notice that you are surrounded by, infused with, and kept in life by love— God's love, that beating heart of the universe."[7]

And once you notice that divine love, what choice do you

have but to pay attention to the One who loves you? If you truly believed that you were loved with that kind of love, what else could you possibly want to do but listen?

"Thick skin, tender heart."

I don't even remember anymore what prompted Dan to say that to me one day. But the gentle admonition that he offered me has since become something of a mantra, one that I've shared with friends and loved ones.

"Thick skin, tender heart."

You never want to toughen up so much that you lose your tender heart, the part of you that experiences and processes pain and compassion and love. Sometimes you have to remember that it's okay not to embody Teflon. Sometimes you have to remind yourself to stay human, which is to say, you have to remind yourself that God gave you a heart for a reason—a heart that is not impervious to all manner of provocation, a heart that takes in external stimuli and responds to them, a heart that throbs with the full range of emotion. Sometimes you have to remind yourself that it is okay, and not just okay but normal and right and good, to feel hurt when someone calls you names or questions your faith.

I'm just as uncomfortable with uncertainty and emotional exposure as the next person, but I also know that just about every sociological study on the subject shows that meaningful connection requires risk and vulnerability, and you can't argue with that data. (Facts!) And so, much to my discomfort, my study and my reading have continually pointed me beyond the safe little stacks of books on my kitchen table and my nightstand into the wild, unpredictable world of lived, human experience, where loving God and loving my neighbor means showing up, risking disappointment, getting things wrong, and praying to a God I'm not certain is even there.

I return again and again to Jesus, who made himself vulnerable too. When he was asked about the fundamental elements of the faith, he replied with uncharacteristic directness—none of the puzzling opacity of the parables, none of the infuriating questions in response to the disciples' questions. He just quoted the Shema.

So in those tough moments, I try to return myself to that love. When someone calls me a Jezebel for the umpteenth time, I try to return myself to that love. When I've made a mess of things on Twitter, I do my best to apologize—and I try to return myself to that love. When someone deems me a "Honey-Boo-Boo publicity whore and embarrassment to the church"—I have to admit, that one was new and different—I try to return myself to that love.

But then you might also want to find some really good dark chocolate or pour yourself a glass of expensive wine.

## 6

# JONATHAN EDWARDS IS NOT MY HOMEBOY

By the time Eve Ettinger[1] was twelve years old, they had developed a standard answer to the question "How are you doing?"

Friend and stranger alike received the same unexpected response.

"Better than I deserve!" Eve said.

As they explained in a guest post on my blog, Eve learned this response from a popular American pastor and denominational leader famous for using the line on bewildered baristas and telemarketers as a way of reminding himself and others that, in his words, "I am never doing worse than I deserve because I deserve hell."[2] Eve's church in Virginia was part of a network of churches under the leadership of this pastor, who teaches a form of Calvinism in the tradition of American Puritanism that emphasizes human depravity and God's wrath against sin. So whether a day began with pancakes and syrup or with slammed doors and painful spankings, Eve's response remained the same, for they believed that "even your worst day is better than what you, a sinner, deserve."[3]

> A dysfunctional home life is better than what you, a sinner, deserve.
> Regular beatings are better than what you, a sinner, deserve.
> Cancer is better than what you, a sinner, deserve.
> Rape is better than what you, a sinner, deserve.

With the help of friends and therapists, Eve found a way out of the church of her youth and onto the path to healing. Yet years of internalized messages about their inherent unworthiness took a toll.

"I try to avoid using the word 'deserve' now," Eve writes. "'Deserve' is a dirty word."[4]

Few churches make it as explicit as Eve's, but the teaching that our sin renders us unworthy of God's love and therefore undeserving of any goodness or joy in life has wormed its way into Christian thinking through the years, helped along by extreme interpretations of the doctrine of total depravity. While the Bible speaks of sin primarily in terms of missing the mark or falling short of the glory of God, much of Western Christianity came to adopt stark, totalizing language to describe humans as possessing a holistic, unalterable sin nature, which article 11 in section I of the Lutheran Book of Concord characterizes as the "entire absence of all good . . . a deep, wicked, horrible, fathomless, inscrutable, and unspeakable corruption of the entire nature and all its powers."[5] (Looks like someone caught a *Real Housewives of New Jersey* marathon while writing theology.)

In one of the most famous sermons in American religious history, eighteenth-century revivalist preacher Jonathan Edwards declared: "The God that holds you over the pit of Hell, much as one holds a spider, or some other loathsome insect, over the fire, abhors you, and is dreadfully provoked; his wrath toward you burns like fire; he looks upon you as worthy of nothing else, but to be cast into the fire; he is of purer eyes than to bear to have you in his sight; you are ten thousand times so abominable in his eyes as the most hateful venomous serpent is in ours."[6]

The message is clear: God hates you. God is disgusted by you. God thinks no more of you than you might think of a pesky insect crushed under your boot. It's certainly a compelling message—members of Edwards's congregations reportedly writhed on the floor in anguish when they heard it. Whether Edwards hyperbolized or meant these words literally, the context has largely been lost to history. What was handed down through the generations was a boiled-down version of this hair-singeing, soul-scarring teaching. Generations later, Eve Ettinger internalized it and I—and millions of other people—experienced a version of it as well.

But is it true?

I grew up with traditional, Western teachings about sin, but unlike Eve, I never believed that the worst thing that happened to me was better than I deserved. The first Bible verse I memorized in AWANA was John 3:16, after all, which famously begins, "For God so loved the world . . ."

That's not to say I never heard about sin. In the Gospel tracts that inevitably snuck into our sacks of Halloween candy—trick or treat?—sin appeared as a wide, bottomless gulf between the stick figure labeled "man" and the stick figure labeled "God," across which the cross of Christ provided the only bridge. In church, I learned that if anyone ever claimed to be sinless, I should quiz them on the Ten Commandments to prove that just one lie, one swear, one moment of jealousy or rebellion or disloyalty, would be enough to separate them from God. My evangelical culture spoke little of systemic or cultural sin, but by the time I reached college I understood intuitively what Tess of the d'Urbervilles meant when she described our world as "a blighted star."[7] In the symphony of my young faith, sin sounded a bit like the bass line, steady and sad and constant, over which the more joyful melodies of grace and redemption occasionally danced.

I thought I possessed a pretty conventional understanding of sin and salvation until I attended an evangelical Christian college in the early 2000s, where, in the wake of the September 11th attacks, Calvinism made a comeback. With the nation confronting the reality of evil, and with the proliferation of

sermons and religious materials online, it seemed as if every serious Christian at my school—or at least every serious Christian
whose facial hair and full-frame glasses made him my "type"—
spent their weekends at the local coffee shop panegyrizing the
wonders of total depravity, unconditional election, and the perseverance of the saints. Conservative midwestern pastors who
preached for forty-five minutes in suits and ties became unlikely
rock stars among my peers, the books of John Piper and Wayne
Grudem selling out at the campus bookstore. One handsome
classmate with a Minnesota accent described himself to me as a
"Christian hedonist," a term straight out of Piper's writing; this
classmate's self-identified chief indulgence consisted not of food
or drink, carnal pleasure or chemical escape, but of studied
meditation on the Westminster Shorter Catechism's charge to
"glorify God, and to enjoy him forever." The September 2006
edition of the evangelical flagship publication *Christianity Today*
boasted a cover story about so-called New Calvinism entitled
"Young, Restless, Reformed." It featured a picture of a young
man wearing a graphic tee that said, JONATHAN EDWARDS IS
MY HOMEBOY.[8]

According to my New Calvinist friends, the biggest problem with contemporary American Christianity was that it in-
dulgently overemphasized God's love to the woeful neglect of
God's wrath. The seeker-sensitive models of church that drew
large crowds with praise bands, worship songs, and uplifting
sermons had led to the "Oprahfication" of Western spirituality, they said. As a result, most people's faith had become too
comfortable, too emotional, too inclusive, and—could there be

anything more damning?—too *feminine*.[9] The surest way to elicit a vigorous eye roll from a New Calvinist was to quote the old adage "God loves you and has a wonderful plan for your life." Such sentiment reeked of the sort of feel-good, navel-gazing, self-satisfying Christianity that undoubtedly sent their homeboy Jonathan spinning in his grave. Words like "worthiness" and sentiments like "You deserve better" belonged to a dominant culture obsessed with self-esteem and secular humanism, not to a true, honorable, self-abnegating faith that put a holy God at its center and our grievous sin in the appropriate spotlight.

Despite all the pomp and patriarchy, I felt strangely drawn to New Calvinism. It wasn't simply because I craved fellowship with this elite band of cultural contrarians. Rather, New Calvinism offered something that my parents could never give me: a consistent theological system that seemed to answer all my questions about God.

> *How could a good and loving God allow so much suffering in the world?*
>
> Because suffering is all that sinners like us deserve.
>
> *What happens to the millions of people who never even had the chance to embrace Christianity due to the circumstances of their birth?*
>
> They are simply not among God's chosen; the fact that any of us receive grace is an undeserved miracle.

*Why are so few chosen?*

The better question might be: Why are *any* of us chosen, given the seriousness of our sin and the punishment we are said to deserve?

*Why do these answers offend my conscience?*

Because my sin nature has so totally corrupted my reason and will, I am incapable of sorting out right from wrong on my own. It only *seems* wrong because I *am* wrong and because I deserve eternal suffering.

This system was comforting in the way that math can be comforting, or the perfect crease, or a row of books neatly arranged. The quintessence of Enlightenment rationalism, the system had its own tidy, self-reinforcing, seemingly airtight and therefore undoubtedly divinely inspired logic.

Yet try as I might, I couldn't stop every cell in my body from reacting with visceral horror at the thought of men, women, and children suffering unending torment in hell at the hands of a raging Father who created them for no other purpose than to suffer, who gave them life only to condemn them to death, who never loved them—and could never love them. I just couldn't stomach it. When John Piper declared the Asian tsunami of 2004 an act of God's judgment, claiming that the tragic deaths of more than 230,000 people were meant to remind us that "what sin deserves is like this, only worse,"[10] I stopped trying to reconcile the theology altogether. I couldn't do it.

The fault lay with my sex, I was told, a long-standing problem traceable all the way back to humanity's earliest days, just after creation. Ever since Eve, this argument went, drawing on that venerable elevation of mind above heart, women have let their emotions obscure the truth. Others blamed my parents. "I know your dad is respected around here," a local Presbyterian pastor chided me. "But do you think maybe he raised you to think too highly of yourself and of all sinful human beings?"

I felt caught in the vibrating tension between two intuitive poles: the sense that sin is a real and destructive force in my life and in the world, and the conviction that every human being is inherently valuable and worthy of love. I wanted to believe that the love of God was not so dissimilar to human love as to render torture, abuse, mass shootings, and drownings all part of God's redemptive plan. But neither did I want the type of soft, sentimental faith the New Calvinists warned me about. So I proceeded with caution, hoping that God really loved the world in a way that felt like love, while avoiding any prayers or meditations that might overindulge that hope and turn my faith into some poor, sappy trope, as if it were the spiritual equivalent of one of Oprah's Favorite Things.

People tend to think that lapses in faith occur after a major crisis or misstep, that we collapse into those devastating spiritual valleys after some precipitous fall from grace. Does grace really exist on a cliff's edge? In my experience, the surest path to religious burnout is through an overabundance of caution and the proliferation of fear. It's hard to take a leap of faith when you're out with your Rolatape measuring distances. So after college, my faith sputtered. I got married, started writing for the local paper, and tried to put all of these questions about sin and worthiness out of my mind. Though I attended church, I checked out emotionally the minute I entered the sanctuary. (That's what I was supposed to do, right? Tone down the feelings?) I read about God, wrote about God, and argued about God, but I couldn't seem to connect with God in the same way I had as a child. It didn't seem worth the risk.

In the midst of this spiritual desert, on the feast day of Saint Francis of Assisi, I stumbled upon a poem by Daniel Ladinsky drawn from the words of that eccentric saint:

> I think God might be a little prejudiced.
> For once He asked me to join Him on a walk
> through this world,
> and we gazed into every heart on this earth,
> and I noticed He lingered a bit longer
> before any face that was
> weeping,
> and before any eyes that were
> laughing.
> And sometimes when we passed
> a soul in worship,
> God too would kneel
> down.
> I have come to learn: God
> adores His
> creation.[11]

*God adores His creation.*

The beauty of that image, the scandal of it, caught my breath. I slammed the book shut and wiped away a rush of sudden, hot tears.

These words seemed dangerous, heretical even. They seemed too good to be true. And yet did they not call to mind the poetry of the prophets, who spoke to Israel of a God who "will exult over you with loud singing," who has "called you by name," and who has "loved you with an everlasting love"?[12] Did they not sound like the God of Hebrew Scripture, who soared over creation in the beginning and declared every flower and fish and tree and human in it "good"? Did they not echo the letters of a saint who proclaimed that "neither death, nor life, nor angels, nor rulers, nor things present, nor things to come, nor powers, nor height, nor depth, nor anything else in all creation, will be able to separate us from the love of God"?[13] Did they not sound like Jesus, who, through the smooth laminate of my AWANA workbook, first told me that "God *so loved* the world"?

That poem cracked open a longing inside me that had been shut up for years. It was a longing for love, and not just generic love—because nobody wants to be loved in general—but specific love, the kind of love that sees every complicated and intimate detail of a person's life and delights in it and embraces it. I didn't want to be pitied or tolerated by the God who made me, as if I were a battered old teddy bear that had lost an eye and its appeal; I wanted to be cherished by God. I didn't want God to look at me and "only see Jesus"; I wanted God to see *me*, all of me, all of what God had created and all of what life had wrought. And I wanted the same for my fellow human beings—every face weeping, every eye laughing—who, despite Jonathan Edwards's sermons and John Piper's blog posts, I still believed to be worthy of God's love simply because they existed. All 7.5 billion of them.

As it turns out, this desire to be loved and to belong is not unique to emotionally needy writers spoiled by their parents. It is inherent to us all. It helps make us human.

You'll find evidence of this in Brené Brown's research. She has spent the last twenty years studying the characteristics of people who, regardless of life circumstances, exhibit resilience. Using a qualitative method known as grounded theory research, Brown conducted thousands of interviews with people spanning all sorts of cultural and socioeconomic backgrounds to conclude that "a deep sense of love and belonging is an irreducible need for all women, men, and children."[14]

"We are biologically, cognitively, physically, and spiritually wired to love, to be loved, and to belong," Brown writes in *The Gifts of Imperfection*. "When those needs are not met, we don't function as we are meant to. We break. We fall apart. . . . We hurt others. We get sick." Her research concluded that the key to connection is no mystery: "I realized that only one thing separated the men and women who felt a deep sense of love and belonging from the people who seemed to be struggling for it. That one thing was the belief in their worthiness. . . . If we want to fully experience love and belonging, we must believe that we are worthy of love and belonging."[15] In fact Brown defines wholehearted living as "a way of engaging with the world from a place of worthiness."[16]

It's important to note that Brown uncovered these findings while researching the corrosive effects of shame. Shame is the ultimate connection killer, for it tells us that our flaws make us unworthy of love. Like many researchers and psychologists, Brown draws a distinction between shame and guilt, noting that the former focuses on *being* while the latter focuses on *behavior.* While guilt says, "I did something bad," shame says, "I *am* bad." Studies suggest a healthy dose of guilt can actually inspire us to make healthier choices, but shame, as a rule, proves counterproductive.

For people of faith, and especially for Christians, this research raises some important questions: Does any claim to our inherent worthiness contradict religious teaching and the witness of our sacred texts? Can we deal honestly with our sins without internalizing shame? Does our belief system require that we see ourselves as nothing more than loathsome insects, deserving only to be swept by tsunami waves into the fires of hell? Or can we, too, engage the world from a place of worthiness?

Many of us have been talked out of that hope by a parent, a Sunday school teacher, a pastor, or perhaps even our very own fragile selves. In some way or another, many of us have become convinced that we will never be worthy of love—because of our sin, because of our humanity, and because of something that happened in a mysterious garden a long time ago.

Still, I think, deep in their hearts, most people want to believe that they are somehow worthy of love and belonging, that their worst day of suffering or their best day of wholeheartedness is not better than they deserve. I think most people yearn for a God who not merely tolerates but also adores God's creation. I think most people still long for a God who kneels down.

PART TWO

# ESSAYS ON THE CHRISTIAN LIFE

## 7

# BEGINNING AGAIN
# WITH LOVE

t's a story we think we know.

The perfect paradise, free of conflict, fear, and death. The naked couple, in love and unashamed. An apple, a snake, a terrible mistake. The birth story of sin and the moment of our collective separation from God.

For so many Christians, the tale of Adam and Eve in the Garden of Eden carries with it far more significance than the average ancient Near Eastern creation myth. Many of us learned in Sunday school that the third chapter of Genesis depicts an earth-shattering event called the Fall, in which the first humans, born into a world without sin or death, succumb to the temptation of Satan. And with their one act of disobedience, with that bite into a piece of fruit, they unleash the forces of evil into the cosmos.

This is the story that explains why we suffer, why we fight wars, why hurricanes and earthquakes ravage the earth, why we lie, why we can't agree on politics, why we divorce, why we get old, why we die. It explains the cruel things we say to one another and the brutal things we say to ourselves. It is the historical footnote to those harmful thoughts that seem to sprout from nowhere. It is the reason why God feels so distant at times. It tells us who we are and what we are destined to do. It marks us as unworthy.

. . . Or so we think.

Shared as a common origin myth by all three Abrahamic faiths—Judaism, Christianity, and Islam—the story of Adam and Eve has been subjected to so much projection through the centuries, it's almost impossible to read it without seeing things that aren't there. For example, Western art and imagination favor the apple as the forbidden fruit, but in the story itself, the fruit of the Tree of the Knowledge of Good and Evil is never named. (We might have a translator, Jerome, to blame here; many scholars believe he was punning it up when he was working on the Vulgate Bible and called the Tree of the Knowledge of Good and Evil the *bonum et malum*. The Latin *malum* can mean three different things: "evil," "fruit" generically, and "apple" specifically.)

Contrary to popular embellishment, the Bible never describes the garden or creation as "perfect" (a concept borrowed more from Plato than the Bible). Rather, it describes the earth and everything in it as "good," "very good," and "blessed."

Nowhere does the text claim that before the man and woman ate the forbidden fruit, death was not part of the natural cycle of growth and decay necessary to make a garden green, nor does it say the couple were promised immortality if they obeyed. Even the crafty serpent is never explicitly identified as Satan. Perhaps most significantly, nothing in the first three chapters of Genesis, or in the rest of Hebrew Scripture, for that matter, suggests that the choice made by Adam and Eve in the Garden of Eden permanently and negatively altered their nature, forever damaging the image of God within them and transmitting that damage like a congenital disease to every person on Earth. In fact, the word "sin" is nowhere to be found.

The story that supposedly defines our relationship with God fails even to get a second reference in the entirety of the Old Testament. It is never addressed by Jesus. And it appears nowhere in the historic creeds of the Christian faith.

Neither Judaism nor Eastern Christianity has ever held to the doctrine of original sin; their adherents do not believe that the choice of Adam and Eve permanently altered the nature of all human beings. And ministers and scholars across the theological spectrum have long questioned the notion that Genesis 3 describes a single, historic moment in which humankind somehow lost its connection to God. Such a reading relies on flights of theological fancy far beyond the text itself and diminishes what is established at the beginning of Genesis— that God created the world out of love, blessed it and called it good, and impressed upon each person the very image and likeness of the divine.

"God calls us good and beloved before we are anything

else," explains pastor and theologian Danielle Shroyer in her book *Original Blessing: Putting Sin in Its Rightful Place*. Shroyer's reading of the creation story offers a much-needed lifeline to those of us who are drowning in the certainty of our unworthiness. "Sin is not at the heart of nature; blessing is," she continues. "And that didn't stop being true because Adam and Eve ate fruit in the garden. In fact, it has never stopped being true."[1]

Notice that when God places the first humans in the garden, God situates them beneath the shade of a sprawling Tree of Life—an image that evokes the interconnectedness of all living things. God's involvement in the life of the garden and its inhabitants is intimate, almost humanlike. The text reports that God strolled through the grounds "at the time of the evening breeze."[2] And like children exploring a safe and loving home, Adam and Eve enjoy their connection to creation, to God, and to each other, free of worry and shame. God tells them they can eat from any tree they want, except the Tree of the Knowledge of Good and Evil. Eating from that tree leads to the opposite of life; it leads to death.

As a kid, I always found this curious—that God would forbid Adam and Eve from eating from the Tree of the Knowledge of Good and Evil. Isn't that what God's people are supposed to want—to know the difference between right and wrong, good and bad? Aren't we meant to desire wisdom, as Eve did, when she reached for the fruit that promised it?

These questions have intrigued the faithful for centuries, and explain why many biblical scholars characterize the story of Genesis 2–3 as a form of wisdom literature, similar in its themes to the books of Proverbs and Ecclesiastes, which re-peatedly remind readers that knowledge gained apart from God is not true wisdom at all. In biblical literature, wisdom is described as "a tree of life to those who lay hold of her."[3] Those who find wisdom find life, and those who fail to find wisdom "love death."[4] "The fear of the Lord is the beginning of wis-dom," Scripture declares, but knowledge gained for its own sake proves nothing more than "a chasing after the wind."[5]

Perhaps the failure of Adam and Eve, then, isn't their desire to know right from wrong, good from evil, but rather their attempt to gain that knowledge through a convenient shortcut, apart from God. In a sense, they tried to grow up too fast, to shake away the hand of their loving Parent before they were ready to run around on their own. Read in its historical, lit-erary, and religious contexts, perhaps the story of Adam and Eve isn't about a single moment—a great "Fall" that explains the origins of evil and the presence of death in the world—but rather about the many moments in which human beings face a choice between independence and interdependence. It serves as a warning, originally to Israel but also to us, that autonomy is overrated. Trying to go it alone, without the wisdom of our Creator (and to the Israelites, without the law of the Torah to guide them gently toward it), leads to shame and exile, dese-cration and death.

You don't have to be an ancient Israelite to recognize the truth of this, to see how knowledge gained and deployed without wisdom can lead to death. With scientific knowl-edge, humans have created both life-saving vaccines and body-obliterating atomic bombs. With what we know about human psychology, we have healed one another's wounds and exploited one another's weaknesses. With advances in technology, we can both wish our great-aunt a happy birthday from thousands of miles away and call someone we've never met a "bed-wetting feminazi" on Twitter. (Still trying to figure out that one.) Even our knowledge of Scripture has been used to advance righteous and noble causes as well as to justify all sorts of violence, oppression, and exclusion. The Tree of Knowledge must always grow next to the Tree of Life, their roots intertwining, lest in our striving for comprehension we forget to honor the sacredness of our connection—to God, to one another, and to all of life.

The Dutch-Brazilian priest and theologian Carlos Mesters wrote that "to become aware of evil is a shattering experience,"[6] and indeed, immediately after rejecting God's direction and eating the fruit, Adam and Eve sense that something is wrong. "The eyes of both of them were opened, and they knew that they were naked," the story says.[7] But rather than turn away from the pair as they scramble for fig leaves to cover their bodies, God moves *toward* them in their vulnerability. God seeks them out. At no point does the ground tremble as a gulf opens between God and the humans God created. Even when God banishes the pair from the Garden of Eden as part of a series of "curses" directed at the snake, the woman, and the man, the point seems to be to protect them and the world from the consequences of their decision.

Like other creation narratives of the time, the story of Adam and Eve is etiological, explaining how things came to be. It describes in fanciful, nonliteral terms why childbirth is painful and why farming is hard and why snakes crawl on the ground. It helped the people of Israel understand why they needed the law of the Torah. It serves as an epic coming-of-age tale. It's not a story about how humans lost their worth; it's a story about how humans lost their innocence. And most important, it's not a story about how God turned away from creation but rather a story about how God, in God's relentless way, moved toward creation while giving people the freedom to make choices, to test boundaries, to rebel, to wreak havoc, to grow up.

The stories we tell about ourselves matter, and if the primary story we tell about ourselves is that, ever since the garden, our sin nature makes us incapable of doing good and unworthy of love and belonging, then we will live like people who are incapable of doing good and unworthy of love and belonging. If, on the other hand, the primary story we tell about ourselves is that we are God's good and beloved creation, made in the image of the divine and worthy of love no matter our sins and failures, then we will live into that reality and seek it out in one another.

Shroyer suggests replacing "sin nature" with "human nature" for a more biblical and honest accounting of our moral state. "We are not born innocent, since we are born into a conflicted world," she writes. "But we are not born sinful, either. We're born human, and within us lies the potential for both creation and destruction, both blessing and curse. To be human is to be capable of both incredible good and terrifying evil. If we deny either side of that potential, we're living unaware."[8]

Now, the guys with the JONATHAN EDWARDS IS MY

HOMEBOY T-shirts might say any description of our humanity that acknowledges some goodness in it takes too high a view of things. But I'm just not convinced the biggest problem facing the world today is that we are too sure of our own belovedness and the inherent beauty of God's creation. In fact, I daresay our greatest sins, both personal and corporate, emerge from a denial of that reality. Embracing God's love for creation isn't some trite form of positive self-talk; it's not a wave of the hand that says, "Everything's good," or, "We're all fine." It's the complicated, challenging, and unwavering conviction that every single person is created in the image of God and loved by God, even your enemies, and even you.

Operating from that conviction is no walk in the Edenic park, let me tell you. In my experience, centering my worldview and ethics around the inherent worth and belovedness of all of creation makes me even more attuned to the seriousness of doing harm to God's beloved. It makes me even more aware of my own capacity for destruction and desecration. Centering our conversations about sin around God's love rather than our depravity raises the stakes, for it means that salvation isn't just about managing our own personal sins; it's also about restoring health and wholeness to all of creation.

As activist and theologian Lisa Sharon Harper puts it, "humanity is made in the image of God. . . . To slap another human is to slap the image of God. To lie to another human is to lie to the image of God. To exploit another human is to exploit the image of God . . . to commit acts of physical, emotional, psychological, sexual, political, and economic violence against fellow humans is to attempt to crush the image of

God on earth." Harper continues by explaining that "sin is not about the personal imperfection of the self. Rather, sin is any act that breaks any of the relationships God declared very good in the beginning."[9]

Starting with God's love like this helps us put God's wrath into perspective. There's a common misunderstanding among many Christians that God is equal parts love and wrath, and the trick is to strike a theological balance between the two. But the Bible doesn't teach this. The Bible teaches that God's entire essence is love.

"Beloved, let us love one another," John wrote, "because love is from God; everyone who loves is born of God and knows God. Whoever does not love does not know God, for God is love."[10]

God *is* love.

"God is love," he wrote, "and those who abide in love abide in God, and God abides in them."[11]

Whatever wrath God feels about injustice and our complicity in it, whatever anger God directs at the human capacity for evil, flows out of love. God gets angry at sin because sin hurts the people and the creation God loves. God rages against child abuse and rape, racism and white supremacy, homophobia and biphobia and transphobia, ableism and ageism, misogyny and exploitation, cruelty and consumerism, because these sins denigrate the dignity of those whom God made and dishonor the beauty of the world that God made. Because these sins defy God's love. Because these sins go against God, who is love and who, in and through that love, created everything that we see, including you and including me.

# 8

# FROM DEATH TO LIFE

I am an Enneagram 3.

I know there are detractors who believe the Enneagram is just astrology for Christians and others who say things like "You couldn't possibly put me in a box." (I'd say they're either a 4 or a 1.) But this personality tool has been helpful in framing my strengths, weaknesses, and proclivities.

Enneagram 3s are the people you hate to play board games with, because we really, really, really like to win. No one turns an evening of fun and frivolity into a *Hunger Games*–style fight to the death like an Enneagram 3. When we are healthy, 3s are productive, persuasive, and inspiring. When we are unhealthy, we become obsessed with success and with winning and with destroying the competition. We simply *cannot let that Facebook argument go*. According to Don Richard Riso and

Russ Hudson, creators of The Enneagram Institute, "Threes want to win, not so much for the things winning will buy, or for the power and feeling of independence that it will bring. They want to succeed because they are afraid of disappearing into a chasm of emptiness and worthlessness if they don't."[1]

That sounds right to me. If I don't win this—this on-line argument, this theological debate, this last round of Bananagrams—I will in fact vanish into a veritable Grand Canyon of irrelevance and unimportance. I will be revealed as the nobody I believe I am, sucked into the black hole where things that have no value go.

When I examine my life as a Christian, I find there are many things I am willing to sacrifice to follow Jesus—because, I won't lie, there's a small part of me that's still determined to win at following Jesus. I'll sacrifice my time. I'll sacrifice my treasure. I'll even sacrifice (some aspects of) my reputation.

Am I willing to relinquish the chance at having the last word in a fierce debate? Am I willing to let someone else "win" for the sake of maintaining the relationship? Am I willing to give someone else the apparent upper hand for the sake of the Gospel?

Not so much.

Sociologists tell us that winning an argument is actually a terrible way to change someone's mind. Turns out life is more than just an extended Bananagrams tournament. Winning, in other words, isn't really winning, at least not if one's goal is conversion—even just conversation rather than conquest. In fact, it tends to produce the opposite of our desired effect, because when people feel as if their worldview is being threatened, they become protective and defensive, digging in their proverbial heels even more. As Jonathan Haidt explains so brilliantly in *The Righteous Mind*, people are far more likely to be persuaded when they feel seen and heard, when they believe their own argument has been fairly presented, and if they are confronted by a story.

Sociologists are of course stumbling upon something Jesus knew better than anyone. He understood that if you want to upend a community's worldview, you have to tell stories, connecting truth to everyday experiences, as he does in the parables. You have to behave in unexpected ways, which, in his case, included turning the other cheek and healing on the Sabbath and hanging out with sinners. You have to be willing to share meals with other people, sitting with them and hearing their stories too. And you might even have to cede some ground, surrender some pride, sacrifice some honor—dying, as it were, a thousand little deaths.

Jesus took this last one to an extreme. He rejected prestige. Though he wasn't afraid to engage with the powerful, he was much more likely to linger amidst the lowly and dine with the disfavored.

Jesus was even willing to die on a cross—an act of radical faithfulness that humiliated and disarmed the Empire by revealing its ultimate emptiness and its fundamental powerlessness in the face of love. Which leads me to wonder: What else must die for the sake of life and for the sake of love?

I went to elementary school at Parkway Christian School in Birmingham, Alabama, and the most important thing you need to know about PCS is that every year it gave out a very special award. It went to one boy and one girl in each classroom. It was voted on by fellow students, so it came with the gloss of popular recognition. And it was called the Best Christian Attitude Award.

You might have heard me tell this story before, because I'm still pretty proud that I won it. Being the religious overachiever that I was—and, I confess, still am—I coveted that award. I hated it when someone else won it. Which may say something about whether my Christian attitude was really the best, but whatever.

Beginning in fifth grade, I developed entirely legal strategies to win the election. I let boys cut in front of me at the water fountain (generosity). I told the entire class that I wanted to serve as a missionary in Africa when I grew up, giving my life to Christ (devotion). I was the first to answer the teacher's questions about the Bible stories that we were studying (scholarship). I promised to pray for everyone's ailing hamsters (service).

Sure enough, it worked. I won the Best Christian Attitude Award four years running. And I've said before and I will say again that I probably would have won it more if my parents hadn't moved my sister and me to a public school, where the award's existence would have violated the Establishment Cause of the First Amendment to the US Constitution.

When I read stories about the Apostle Peter, I can't help

but think that the poor guy felt at times as if he might be on the cusp of winning his own Best Christian Attitude Award. (My empathetic posture toward Peter, which could be characterized for award purposes as charity, might be based in the truth that I never really had to imagine him as my competition, since, as I said, one boy and one girl got the honor in each classroom.)

As Peter lived in Jesus's orbit, religious leaders were turning against Jesus. People around town were talking. Some were saying that Jesus was a prophet. John the Baptist had recently been beheaded, so others were suggesting that he might be John resurrected. Still others were saying that Jesus was some crazy guy ranting about some kingdom—which kingdom?— being "at hand," which sounds just bizarre.

Then, according to the eighth chapter of the Gospel According to Mark, Jesus asks his disciples, "Who do you say that I am?"

In my imagination, Peter shoots his arm toward the sky more quickly than anyone (except me), his hand quivering for his rabbi Jesus's attention. Peter's entire body screams, *Oh! Oh! Pick me! I know! You are the Messiah! You are the liberator we've been waiting for! You're the one who will vanquish all our enemies, establish a throne, and rule forever!* Peter is already mentally footnoting each line and cross-referencing with Scripture.

Jesus, ever the disappointing leader, fails to respond with appropriate enthusiasm to Peter's obvious abundance of knowledge. Instead, he says to his disciples: "Don't tell anyone." Then he follows that up with some talk about how he is going to face intense suffering, waves of rejection, and even death at the hands of his enemies.

When Peter understandably objects—"Don't talk like that!" you can imagine him saying. "We are not going to let that happen!"—Jesus replies by granting Peter what amounts to the *opposite* of the Best Christian Attitude Award: "Get behind me, Satan!" he says.[2]

You never want to hear your rabbi or your friend compare you to the devil himself. It might just cramp your self-esteem momentarily. The rebuke stings—and Jesus isn't even done yet. In front of everyone, he accuses Peter of thinking in human terms, not divine ones. He suggests that Peter is being shortsighted about how God works. And he implies that Peter believes the key to a meaningful life is to avoid pain, to stave off trial, to cheat death at all costs.

Jesus sees things differently. Our God, he says, works not through the traditional human mechanisms of power, control, and military might but rather through suffering, sacrifice, and servanthood. This kingdom will come not through powerful armies riding in on their prized warhorses but by way of a singular savior lumbering in on the back of someone else's donkey and sitting atop someone else's cloak. This king's reign will be marked not by demonstrations of brute force or acts of terror but by gestures of healing and whispers of mercy, touches of tenderness and waves of grace. This people's enemies will not be vanquished; they will be loved.

If you want to follow me, you have to prepare not to win but to lose, Jesus says. You might have to lose your need to be right, your lust for blue ribbons, your desire to be first. You—as well as all your claims to the Best Christian Attitude Award—might even have to die.

I can just imagine how Peter might have felt after Jesus said those words: "Get behind me, Satan." The heat rising in his face, the prickle on his skin, the gurgle in his gut—oh, the embarrassment! Who wants to be publicly rebuked by anyone, let alone the man who might be the Messiah?

I suspect there was something deeper, though. I sense that Peter also might have felt something beyond humiliation. Maybe I'm just projecting, but I wonder whether Peter also felt shame.

Sometimes in the Hebrew Bible, the devil is known as *ha Satan*, which translates in English to "the Accuser." No matter what you believe about the devil or about Satan, whether you believe it to be an actual being, a fallen angel, the human forces of evil, or the shadow side of our own selves, we all know the voice of the Accuser. The voice of shame that mutters in our ears, the voice that somehow finds the express lane into our hearts and heads, the voice that identifies that deeply hidden, deeply rooted insecurity and toys with it, amplifies it, multiplies it—that is the voice of the Accuser. The voice of attribution directed at me, which tells me that I am the worst thing that I have done—that is the voice of the Accuser.

To be clear: the voice of the Accuser is not the voice of one's conscience. My conscience says, *You shouldn't have sent that tweet, because you were being an ass*, and *You were rude to your coworker. Maybe it's a good idea to apologize for being a jerk.* My conscience is the sensible, righteous voice that helps remind me that I need to feel convicted of my sin. As Paul writes, we all have sinned and fall short of the glory of God. This is the human condition that afflicts each and every one of us..

When I speak about the voice of the Accuser, I'm talking about the devastating, deceptive messages that play on repeat within us. They fixate not on what we might have *done* but on how awful we *are*. That's something profoundly different from a rightly guilty conscience. It's shame.

If our sense of ego needs to die for us to truly live, even more so must our sense of shame. So does our unwitting allegiance to the voice of the Accuser—a voice that tells us we're unworthy and that we can never be loved.

It's one thing to say that Jesus was willing to die. The question many of us have wrestled with is slightly different: Why did Jesus *have* to die?

In my childhood understanding of sin and Jesus's intervention, Christ substituted his beauty for my ugliness, his perfection for my flaws. It was as if the mere thought of me would be so unbearable and enraging to a holy God that my only salvation would be if someone held up a photo of me and God somehow saw a picture of Jesus instead. Despite God's omnipotence, omniscience, and omni–everything else, was the very sight of me so bad?

So many hymns and songs concretize this understanding of God's anger, wrath, and utter disappointment—until Jesus. There's "Nothing but the Blood of Jesus": "Naught of good that I have done / Nothing but the blood of Jesus." Or "In

Christ Alone": "Till on that cross as Jesus died / The wrath of God was satisfied."

I am sure that some critic out there will read this and think, *Oh, there she goes again—Rachel Held Evans with her heretical ways, Rachel Held Evans elevating humanity and diminishing the divine, Rachel Held Evans tempting the vulnerable with her confusions.* If it's heretical to ask questions about the nature of God's love or the love of God's nature, then let me be a heretic. If it's heretical to muse about the incongruence of a patient God who exists beyond time being infuriated by my little errors, then let me be a heretic. If it's heretical to wonder what the proper pronouns might be for God, then let me be a heretic (once, I used a feminine pronoun for God, and people still point to that as a reason to wish me a hasty death, which makes me wonder how they'll feel when they enter God's full presence someday and learn that God isn't a dude).

I'm just trying to see humanity for what it is—and God for who God is. And better the confusion that vulnerability might engender and the lack of clarity—one might more charitably call it humility—about atonement theories than the false certainty that has kept so many bound to their self-loathing and their sense of being unlovable to God.

To be clear, I'm not trying to construct a new certainty, a more enlightened fundamentalism, to replace the old versions. That would just be a slightly prettier idol than the one we had before. My hope instead is to urge us toward faithful wondering: What if some of the stories we've been telling ourselves, well intentioned as they might be, should be shelved as fiction? What if those narratives need to be put to death so that something more nourishing, something centered on holy flourishing, something truer, might live?

We are not the first to go this way. In the Jewish tradition, there's a long history of faithful wondering. It's summarized in the midrash, ancient commentaries by the rabbis that contain their speculations about what lies off the page of Scripture, about all the details that didn't make the main scroll.

"Midrash" means "study" or "searching out." In the Jewish rabbinical tradition, this type of learning has always been a group effort. "Through communal reading of Scripture with homiletical commentary and translation, community was formed, reformed and advanced," writes Rabbi Burton Visotzky, midrashic expert and Hebrew Bible scholar. "Midrash was to the Rabbis of old the primary means of hearing God's voice speak through the Word of Scripture."[3]

Midrash was never meant to concretize one particular understanding of a particular verse or a particular part of Scripture. While it sought to uncover ancient truths, it was also relentlessly open to contextualizing the sacred text for a new generation. "Earlier comments were passed on, modified, retold, so that the Bible became a patchwork quilt of text, with a verse of Scripture at the center and the various interpretations of the verse radiating outward to form the fabric," Visotzky says. "This quilt of scriptural interpretation offered warmth to all who sheltered under it."[4]

This image of reading the Bible as helping to construct a quilt, then crawling under it together, might shock those who have experienced Scripture as a bludgeon or a club. Maybe the voice of the Accuser has told us that we are incapable of questioning the text. Maybe the voice of the Accuser has made the audacious claim that God's grace can't encompass our doubts and our interrogations, whether of Scripture or of God's own self. Maybe the voice of the Accuser unravels a thread that we come to identify as fear—fear that we'll get something wrong, fear that a human critique might somehow offend a great God, fear that we are unloved and perhaps even unlovable.

Theologian Leonard Sweet suggests that there might actually be something less than faithful about an uncritical posture toward Scripture. In Jewish culture, he notes, "it's an act of reverence to ask questions of the story. The Jews are confident that the story is strong enough to be tried and tested."[5]

If the story is strong enough to be tried and tested, surely the God who is the ultimate author and inspiration of that story is strong enough—and tender enough—for our explorations too. That's the God I've come to hope in. After all, wasn't this God the same God who was unafraid of death itself, because death had no power over God's love?

In the midrashic tradition, imagination is a key tool for excavating the deeper meanings of holy texts. This is not to suggest that historical context and inherited understandings of sacred poetry and holy prose don't matter. But one's sense of possibility matters too, and if you're so inclined, you might even call it the ongoing work of the Spirit.

"Around the table, a Jewish child has 'That's a good question!' drummed into his or her soul, not 'You don't ask that question,'" Sweet continues. "Questions are as sacred as answers."[6]

So allow me a midrashic moment, a brief wondering: What

if we understood Jesus "descending to the dead" not as going down to hell but as coming down to the unredeemed Earth? What if the realm of the dead wasn't the fiery underworld of our imaginations but rather this aching and weary planet? What if so many of us have been living in dread of hell, not recognizing that this world, with all its evidence of its "bondage to decay," as the Apostle Paul puts it in his letter to the Romans,[7] is the very thing we've feared all along?

I'm wondering whether Jesus's greatest act of solidarity with humanity might have been to take on the long, slow walk toward death that is the reality for each and every person. Only he had the capacity to walk a little farther, empowered by divine love to continue on from the precincts of death into the realm of everlasting life.

Questions only threaten those who have something—some power, some prestige, some veneer of worldly credibility and control—to lose. You hear all manner of bad metaphor when you start asking discomfiting questions about the reality of how things are as opposed to the promise of what might be. For instance, I've always been bothered by the argument that our wonderings and wanderings inevitably send us sliding down that proverbial slippery slope. Where is God in that equation? What happened to our trust in a God who promises, over and over in Scripture, sure footing for those who seek truth?

There's a question behind the question, of course: What are we afraid of? And so often, that lurking fear is a fear of death.

The fear can be an individualized fear, not just of death but also of hell. I've lost count of how many people I've met who told me a story of their parents coming home unexpectedly late, and in those anxious moments waiting for their return, the kid begins to wonder whether the rapture happened and they've been left behind. There are also the soul-wrenching testimonies of heart-pounding, tear-filled, late-night bargaining sessions with God, especially from LGBTQ+ people. You don't soon forget those internal dialogues, in which you promise to stop doing or thinking or feeling this or that—if only God will promise to rescue you from the unquenchable flames.

The fear is a collective one too. There's a lot of talk these days, for instance, about the supposed death of the church. You know how the headlines go: Millennials are leaving. Christians are compromising their values—an accusation that progressives make about conservatives and conservatives make about progressives. Church-attendance numbers are declining.

But death is something empires, not resurrection people, worry about.

In any case, I wonder sometimes whether we're playing at death and calling it life. Maybe we're playing dead when we refuse to ask the big questions. Maybe we're playing dead when we pledge allegiance to American exceptionalism. Maybe we're playing dead when others are suffering and we choose to remain ensconced in our own comfortable denial. Maybe we're playing dead when we repeat the chords of that questionable worship song nine times—eight times too many—without ever analyzing critically what claims it makes about us or our God. Maybe we're playing dead when we fail to consider, when we're at a table or in a sanctuary, who's not at that table or in that sanctuary—who isn't welcome and why. Maybe we're playing dead when we fixate on others' shibboleths yet refuse to interrogate our own.

One of the reasons I'm still a Christian is that this faith liberates me from a fear of death. In doing so, it delves into one of the deepest receptacles of human fear, looks it in the eye, and declares, "I am not afraid."

I am not afraid to name the things that are bringing death to the people I love and calling them wrong.

I am not afraid to say that the church has stifled holy imagination for the sake of the preservation of its own comfort.

I am not afraid to say that many in the church have been agents of death for many women, for queer and trans people, for people of color, for immigrants and refugees, for disabled people, for all manner of minority, for so many who live at the intersections of these identities. Many in the church have not proclaimed good news. They have not declared hope and possibility, justice and welcome.

I am not afraid to say that many parts of the church have been far more concerned with their own comfort than they have been with the flourishing of others.

I am not afraid to say that many segments of the church have invested in power—worldly power, partisan power, compromise-ridden and deal-driven power, in a bid to sustain the status quo.

I am not afraid to say that many of us have seen past the grand facades and hoary rituals of the church, finding an emptiness, a void, that might as well be death.

I am not afraid to say that the walls of the church have been a human-made prison, not a house worthy of God.

I am not afraid to say that, if the church in the US is dying, let it die. Let it die to the old ways of hegemony. Let it die to violence. Let it die to control.

Maybe the church in the US is already dead. But the fear of death is the province of those who do not believe in resurrection. Aren't Christians supposed to be living testimony to the miracle of the resurrection?

So we don't conclude the narrative of the dead or dying church in the graveyard. We look for its resurrection and for its redemption.

> May the church be resurrected to the way of humility.
> May the church be resurrected to the way of curiosity.
> May the church be resurrected to the way of mercy.
> May the church be resurrected to the way of service.
> May the church be resurrected to the way of wholeness.
> May the church be resurrected to the way of the cross.
> May the church be resurrected like Jesus.
> May the church be resurrected by love.

The short, simple, and simply beautiful liturgy of Ash Wednesday, which begins our annual commemoration of Jesus's march toward death, teaches something that nearly everyone can agree on. Whether you are a part of a church or not, whether you believe or you don't, whether you are a Christian or an atheist or an agnostic or someone whose faith experiences far transcend the laughable limits of labels, you know this truth deep in your bones: "Remember that you are dust and to dust you will return."

I find this reminder humbling in the best possible way. It broadens my perspective: I belong to God's creation, to this glorious collection of cells and microbes, trees and flowers, oceans and mountains, forests and fields. I also appreciate its candor: death is a part of life. We need to make time and space not just to acknowledge that reality but also to celebrate it and to grieve it and to wrestle with it and to meditate on it.

In doing so, we will recall a central truth: we are not alone. All of humanity has had to confront this reality—even Jesus himself. And the crucial thing to remember is that with God, death is never the end of the story.

# 9

# THE STEADY WORK
# OF LIVING WATER

'll be the first to admit that I am prone to cynicism. Along
with an iPhone screen cracked from being thrown across
the room, cynicism is undoubtedly one of the chief consequences of being active on social media. There's so much performance around us, so much posturing, that you can easily
begin to wonder whether authenticity even exists anymore.
You grow skeptical of others' mixed motives, in no small part
because you know your own.

Here's the thing: Cynicism is evidence of having given up
and given in. Cynicism is calcified anger. Cynicism is your once-
tender heart now calloused and hardened. Cynicism looks like
strata of sedimentary rock, each layer of protective distance

compressing and solidifying the layer beneath—distance from your pain, distance from others' suffering, distance from the possibility that things might be more complicated than they seem on the surface. Cynicism feels like spiritual Novocain, numbing your whole range of deeply human emotion, because those feelings reflect frightening vulnerability and open up the possibility of yet more disappointment.

In other words, cynicism is totally understandable.

What rescues me from cynicism?

For one thing, there's a dark-chocolate bar I especially like that has little morsels of raspberry hiding throughout. That helps.

Another thing is the reality of hope. Which sounds a whole lot more pious than I mean it to.

It would be dishonest for me not to say I am a Christian when Christianity is the story I will wrestle with forever. There's something about Christianity—and by that, I mean the venerable, beautiful story that has Jesus at its center—I just can't shake. And I don't just mean the parts I like, or the parts that on good days I believe. I mean the whole thing. The whole screwed-up, embarrassing, dysfunctional family of the church is as much a part of my identity as my gender, my nationality, my ethnicity, and my name.

And yet: Why, in the midst of seemingly endless church splits and corruption and discordant debates, am I still a Christian? Why, with a history that includes not only great acts of service and compassion but also the Inquisition, the Crusades, support for slavery, and opposition to civil rights, am I still a Christian? Why, amidst my own persistent doubts that any of this is true—and my fear that if it is, the other guys are ruining it—am I still a Christian? Why do I fight so hard to stave off the cynicism?

For the same reason that, in spite of all that's wrong, it still feels right to splash a bunch of cold water over my kid's little head and baptize him into the family of God.

The story of Jesus being baptized by John the Baptist is one of the most dramatic, otherworldly scenes in the Gospels. As Jesus emerges from the waters of the Jordan River, the heavens were ripped open, Mark says. From that breach in the up-above, the Holy Spirit descends with the gentleness of a dove. Then a voice from on high says, with all the tenderness of a parent: "You are my Son, the Beloved; with you, I am well pleased."[1]

My own baptism had a somewhat different kind of drama.

I was baptized by my father, on the same Sunday as my sister was baptized. I was twelve, and we were attending a very conservative evangelical church in a very conservative evangelical part of the country.

This was a congregation that did not ordain women, that often conflated Republican talking points and Christian ethics, and that was as racially segregated in the 1990s as it had been in the 1960s or the 1860s. This was also the congregation that introduced me to potlucks and the song "Father Abraham." This is the congregation that showed up with homemade chicken soup when my whole family came down with the flu.

This is the congregation that made me feel safe that time the tornado sirens went off. This is the congregation that was the first to tell me that I was a beloved child of God and that instilled in me a profound reverence for Scripture.

I've talked about this before, because I still think it's so hilarious: my biggest concern on the day of my baptism was not that the baptism wouldn't stick but that my clothes would. After going into the water, I imagined, my white T-shirt would cling so tightly to my "stumbling blocks" that I would cause a brother in the congregation to fall into sin. Such are the omnipresent concerns of faithful young evangelical women.

Today, I can reflect on my baptism with another perspective. My baptism reminds me that I am a Christian because Christianity gives me a name that supersedes every other name the world will try to give me. I am a Christian because my baptism has declared that I am a beloved child of God. There is no failure, no sin, no accomplishment, no success that can change that.

In a culture that prizes independence and individualism, Christianity offers an uncomfortable but necessary and insoluble interdependence. The church—by which I mean not just the congregation into which I was baptized or the one that I now call home but rather the universal church that shares one baptism—is a whole network of people spanning two thousand years and every continent and culture on the globe, who love and pray and believe on one another's behalf.

I know I am not alone in feeling a little uncomfortable with the idea of doing things, especially something as significant as baptism, on another's behalf. I thought a lot about this as we considered whether to baptize our little guy in the Episcopal Church, knowing that we as parents would affirm the faith for him—calling him "Christian" on his behalf.

It's not because I think baptism endows some magic charm that guarantees a life of faith. Nor should you read into any of this that one method of baptism is better than another. At least in this aspect of my theology, I'm ecumenical, so sprinkle, splash, or dunk as you see fit.

For me, the strange and ancient ritual of baptism reveals something at the heart of Christian identity.

First and foremost, we are beloved children of God, blessed by layer upon layer of love. Wherever my children's faith and lives may take them—even if it's away from the tradition in which we are raising them—they will know that the act of baptism took place because they were, perhaps clumsily and undoubtedly imperfectly, loved. It was one way in which we, as parents, said to our children, "You are my child, in whom I am well pleased." It was one way in which we, as parents, recognized that God has said and, we hope, will say of us, "You are my child, the beloved; with you, I am well pleased."

Baptism, like communion and confession and the creeds, reminds us that we cannot be Christians on our own. We belong to a community even larger than the one gathered around those rickety folding tables in the fellowship hall, weighed down with Jell-O molds and deviled eggs. It's a family of faith bound together by the same Holy Spirit through whom Christ was conceived and the same Holy Spirit who descended from the heavens like a dove.

Imagine what it might have been like to be present at Jesus's baptism—his dunking not in a chlorinated baptistery under an acoustic-tiled ceiling but in the living waters of the Jordan River under an open sky. Part of a sprawling watershed, these waters are connective; they are fed by snowmelt from Mount Hermon and the surrounding hills, and they in turn feed the Dead Sea. These waters fuel the tamarisk and the rhododendron blossoming on the riverbanks. These waters parch the thirst of ibex and gazelle, which come down to drink. These waters form a flowing buffet for the stork and the kingfisher lurking in the reeds and shrubs. These waters host catfish and carp and bream, tiny mollusks and soft-shelled turtles. These waters irrigate fields of grape and grain and transmogrify into milk and honey.

Baptism, whether in the Jordan's waters or any other, ties us to the cycle of life, through all of which runs water. It reminds us that we belong. It is, of course, much easier to write that out than to reckon with the reality of what belonging to that larger community—to that fractious assemblage of humanity, prone as it is to hurt as much as to help—really means.

Way back in 2003, when people still left voice mails, when "compassionate conservatism" wasn't entirely oxymoronic, and when Mark Zuckerberg's FaceMash was just a mildly sexist college experiment, my classmates chose me to deliver a commencement address at the graduation ceremony of our Christian college. I took the honor seriously—*this was going to be the best, most inspirational, most Christian commencement address*

*by a student ever.* I prepped diligently for weeks amidst all the final exams and the outbreaks of senioritis, working through multiple drafts and soliciting feedback from my parents as well as my professors.

Looking back, the speech was . . . okay. (To this day, I still have nightmares, though, about stepping up to that podium, scanning the crowd, and then looking down to realize that I had left my notes—and my pants—in my dorm room.) My words were, much like I was, brimming with naïve optimism, a youthful sense of possibility, and conviction about what everyone else needed to hear—and what everyone else needed to change.

I told them to go out and change the world.

I told them that, as believers, fully empowered with our four years of training in Christian apologetics, we were uniquely equipped by God and our teachers to speak truth in love.

I told them that the world is dark, and we are called to be the light.

I told them that the world is sick, and we have been blessed to receive the medicine.

I told them that the world is lost, and we know the way.

I told them basically everything you could find on a collection of inspirational Christian posters—you know the ones, with the gauzy pictures of rainbows or the surf crashing against the rocks or that damn cat hanging on by its claws.

It was a different time. While the ash and memory of September 11th still clouded the air and our hearts, US military forces had recently unleashed their "shock and awe" upon Baghdad, and we were convinced that we'd be out of Iraq, victorious, in a matter of months. *Friends* was still on television, and many of us hadn't yet questioned the whiteness of their world—or of our own. Pluto was still a planet.

It was easy for me to be blissfully overconfident and faithfully hubristic. It's not that there was anything inherently wrong with my exhortation to change the world. But looking back, it seems rather incomplete.

If I could do it all over, if I could return to those times when life seemed so much simpler and I thought myself so much smarter, if I could somehow retrofit all the lessons that the thirty-seven-year-old Rachel has learned in the years since into twenty-two-year-old Rachel's mind and body, I'd add something: let the world change you too.

That's exactly what happened after I descended the platform and walked straight into a world that was inhabited not by the straw figures I'd been taught to convert and/or defeat but by real, feeling, flesh-and-blood human beings who didn't stick to whatever depraved script I'd imagined of the atheist or the Muslim, the feminist or the gay, the liberal or the poor, the skeptical or the foreigner. That world is less populated by sharp, black-and-white certainties than by mile after mile and year after year of thick, often impenetrable gray haze.

I thought I was called by God to challenge the atheists, but now I wonder whether many atheists were sent by God to challenge me.

I thought God wanted to use me to show queer people how to be straight. Instead, God empowered queer people to show me how to be a better Christian.

I thought the world needed to hear what I had to say. To

the contrary, I needed the world to help me learn how to listen better.

I thought an integral part of the armor of God, unmentioned by Paul but nonetheless vital, was my own divinely granted strength. What I discovered was the beauty of humility and the willingness to fess up to my profound weakness.

I thought there was just one table in Christ's banquet hall, and the giant, glorious, blazing sign over it read E V A N G E L-I C A L I S M. What I've learned is that the room of feasting is much wider, deeper, and grander than I could have imagined, filled with all manner of tables spilling over with a mind-blowing diversity of dishes and dinnertime companions, rich and spicy curries that my palate can barely handle, and wild and wonderful convictions that my brain can barely process. The conversation at those tables has nourished me, from the feminist coworker who mothered me through my first reporting job to the library stacks that revealed to me the wondrous writing of Richard Rohr and Marilynne Robinson, from the physicist who patiently guided me to an understanding of how evolution actually works to the saints I met on trips to India and Bolivia who were supposed to be blessed by my presence but who ended up blessing me far more with theirs.

I thought the world was essentially a giant patch of weeds, and we, the faithful Class of 2003, the weeders. We have seen that there is certainly evil in the world, and so many varieties of fear and hate, bigotry and prejudice. But I've realized that there is also such abundant life springing up in all sorts of un-likely soil, in the form of protesters who insist that Black lives matter, LGBTQIA+ people who with their very bodies rebuke the insistent messages that they are less than, and survivors who have dared to tell their stories of abuse in the church—wheat enough for a thousand lifetimes of harvests.

I thought the world was waiting for every single one of the answers I had at the ready. As it turns out, I have been blessed by the world's huge, honest, and often unanswerable questions, and every time I have the presence of mind to ask, "What's up with that?" I think I can just about make out God whispering, with a chuckle, "You have no idea."

I'm not arrogant enough to pretend that I gave that speech and graduated from college and instantly realized the error of my previous ways. I resisted at first—and for a while. I feared compromising my beliefs, so I held to them even more tightly and dug my heels in. I remained convinced that it was my job to be Jesus to others, so much so that I missed many chances to let others be Jesus to me—to teach me, to heal me, to sit with me, to break bread with me, to listen to me, to weep with me, to call me to repentance, to love me.

Only later did I realize that perhaps this was the baptism of real life that followed and fulfilled my baptism in water. Perhaps this was the rebirth that had been symbolized by that dunking many years ago—rebirth into a world where the geometry had entirely been realigned, rebirth into a world that was ready to receive me when I was ready to embrace it, rebirth into a world that had so much beauty and goodness and vibrancy to offer because it was created out of love. Perhaps this is the cleansing and the washing that had to happen, once through Christ and again and again through my experiences with God's people.

Water is a force that does its steady work on even the hardest rock—reshaping it, eroding it, marking it. Even impermeable rock can be stained by the minerals water carries. Over time, one way or another, you'll be able to see souvenirs of its presence, evidence that it has left behind to say, "Water was here."

There's a part in the Episcopal Church's baptismal liturgy when the people pray for those who are being baptized, beseeching God to "send them into the world in witness to your love."

*In witness to your love.*

There's a beautiful ambiguity in that statement. Of course there's the implication that those who profess Christ are to bear witness to Christ's love. But one can also read in there an invitation to witness Christ's love that is also at work in the world—to recognize it, to proclaim it, to express our awe and wonder at it.

Like water, Jesus showed up in the unlikeliest of places. When I consider which aspects of his loving ministry we lift up and which we neglect, it strikes me that we often under-emphasize how much he enjoyed feasting, whether it was creating impromptu picnics of fishes and loaves for thousands of friends or accepting invitations to dine in the homes of tax collectors as well as Pharisees. Again and again, we find him at meals, with all motley manner of humanity. "What is infectiously appealing about Jesus is that he likes to celebrate," Amy-Jill Levine writes. "He is consistently meeting people not at the altar but at table, whether as host, guest, or the body and blood to be consumed."[2]

After Christ's departure, the first apostles allowed themselves to be changed by the goodness they encountered in the world. When law-abiding, kosher-eating, Roman-hating Peter encountered a centurion who feared God and gave to the poor, Peter, to his own astonishment, said, "I now realize how true it is that God does not show favoritism but accepts from every nation the one who fears him and does what is right."[3] Then Peter even went so far as to share a meal, as Jesus might have, with his new friend. "You are well aware that it is against our law for a Jew to associate with or visit a Gentile," he said to Cornelius. "But God has shown me that I should not call anyone impure or unclean."[4]

Not anyone.

Only recently have I understood the remarkable sweep of that statement—and the sobering reality that I am still not done yet. When I was a Bible-thumping, churchgoing, know-it-all Republican, God used bleeding-heart, politically correct, question-everything liberals to teach me a little bit more about how to be human and to toy with my concretized notions of who my enemies were. And now that I'm a bleeding-heart, politically correct, question-everything liberal, God still insists on using Bible-thumping, churchgoing, know-it-all Republicans to teach me a little bit more about how to be human and to toy with my concretized notions of who my enemies are.

I have been Peter, and I have been Cornelius. I am still Peter, and I am still Cornelius.

And God is still God. That same patient, long-suffering,

often annoying God seems rather adamantly committed to putting to death my notion that this life is all about being right—and especially that my life is all about me being right. Even as I still believe that God calls us to help change the world, to make it more just, to make it more equitable, to make it more loving, I also believe that God empowers the world to help change us, to make us more just, to make us more equitable, to make us more loving.

The stubbornness of my cynicism, it turns out, is no match for the resilience of God's love or for the steady work of living water.

## 10

# MANY VOICES, MANY MASKS

Writing has taught me a special kind of patience that I am finally learning to apply to my faith. I find myself repeating the same mantras on a day of doubt that I repeat on a day of writer's block: Be patient. Don't rush it. Live the questions. Let this play out.

I think you can apply the same principles to reading. I consider myself fortunate that I was an English major. Studying literature teaches you that there is often nothing "plain" or "clear" about a text. It was always written in a particular context, almost always for a particular context. Interrogation is part of the work. So is empathy—for the writers as well as for other readers.

It puzzles me that it should be any different with the Bible. If we respect this holy book, should we not ask *more* questions of it, not fewer? Do we not engage more deeply with those—and those things—we love, not less?

For so many people, though, the Bible transforms from sacred text into stumbling block once they start interrogating it. It reminds me of my son, who has been in that phase of responding to every single thing out of my mouth with one word: "Why?" (Somehow my answers never seem as compelling to him as Daniel Tiger's.)

Your confidence in the veracity of Scripture might collapse under the accumulated weight of too many whys. But your confidence isn't your god—and Scripture isn't your god either. Scripture tells us about God and points us toward God and testifies about others' encounters with God, but it doesn't contain the entirety of God or even of the story of God. And God, I have to believe, *can* handle a million whys and more. In fact, God invites them, because there's something beautiful about wholehearted pursuit of truth and something hopeful about the earnest desire to understand the One in whom we find our source and our sustenance.

I remember the sense of invitation and joy I felt when I learned that the word "disciple" doesn't mean "expert" or "preacher," "lecturer" or "leader." Instead, it derives from the Latin word *discere*—"to learn." We're learners. We're all in process, all just partway through our studies, all nowhere near the completion of our educations. And it gives me no small amount of comfort to witness how patient Jesus was with his hapless disciples—Thomas, who doubted, and Nathanael, who was sharp-tongued; fickle Peter and finance-challenged Philip ("Six months' wages would not buy enough bread for each of them to get a little," he said, as Jesus prepared to feed the five thousand[1]). We're called to be learners at the feet of the Master Teacher, slowly beginning to understand exactly what the life of faith means.

Our God is the Word made flesh, not the word printed on the page. And we commit a grievous error when we confuse what we consider to be divinely inspired text with the divine itself. People have been harmed by Christians' treatment of Scripture as a hermetically sealed box, to be opened only gingerly and carefully by those approved (it's worth asking by whom) to handle its contents. Lives spiritual but also physical—have been lost because of mistaken ideas about biblical claims and idolatrous allegiances to "Scripture-based" systems.

In college, I read Alfred, Lord Tennyson. His poem "In Memoriam A. H. H." is a particular favorite of mine. Tennyson wrote it amidst tremendous grief, after one of his close friends, Arthur Henry Hallam, died unexpectedly at the age of twenty-two from a brain hemorrhage.

In the aftermath of Hallam's death, Tennyson wrestles in this poem with his own doubts and his own despair. It's a remarkable, extended, and public journey through difficult emotional and spiritual terrain, examining friendship and faith. While the poem is most famous for the line "'Tis better to have loved and lost / Than never to have loved at all," it's this little collection of verse that I find especially timely:

Our little systems have their day;
They have their day and cease to be:
They are but broken lights of thee,
And thou, O Lord, art more than they.

For better or worse, the stories of Scripture are interwoven with my story, right down to my very name. In Sunday school when I was seven, the teacher pulled out a big book of names, searching for each of ours. I was informed that my name means "ewe." I went home from church crying that day, crushed by the conviction that my parents had taken one look at my naked newborn body and declared it disgusting. Learning a ewe is simply a female sheep did little to lift my spirits, especially because I had also found out that my friend Sarah's name meant "princess."

The truth was much more mundane and much less dramatic. (Welcome to my relationship with my long-suffering parents.) As my dad tells the story, he and my mom just liked the sound of the name Rachel. Because our last name, Held, is short and monosyllabic, they also wanted a slightly longer first name that was unlikely to be shortened. ("Naturally," he says, "it was affectionately shortened to Rach.") My middle name, Grace, came from my great-grandmother and also honored the biblical notion of grace.

Still, whatever my parents' inspiration, there's no escaping the fact that the name Rachel is a biblical one. So rather than trying to sever the threads of my life from those of the sacred text, I hope to embrace and understand how they might be interwoven.

Sometimes I read the biblical account of Rachel, and even as I thrill at her rich and complex character, I shy from any direct comparisons to her. I certainly would never have settled for being anyone's junior wife, even if some readings of the text suggest that she was Jacob's preferred partner.

One of my favorite details about Rachel is one that most of us miss: When we meet her in Genesis 29:9, she's a shepherd. Only one other named woman in Scripture (Zipporah, who will become Moses's wife) tends flocks, even though it was customary in many ancient Near Eastern cultures for girls to help with the livestock. It's an inconvenient detail for those advocates of biblical womanhood who would rather keep the wife indoors, tending the hearth and making home.

The Rachel of my imagination enjoys a remarkable degree of autonomy, at least in comparison to the conservative stereotype of the biblical wife. I picture her holding a rough-hewn staff, walking through meadows of ryegrass and clover, goats braying and sheep bleating as they trail after their guardian. She hums a little tune to herself as she lifts her tanned face toward the warmth of the sun. From a patch near her sandaled feet, she plucks a stem of wild fenugreek, its fresh herbaceousness giving her nose a break from her gamy flock. Occasionally, she tucks herself into the shade of an old oak tree, guzzling water from the pouch slung across her hips. Out here in these hills, Rachel is free—free to dream, free to wander, free to question, free to be.

She's willful and resourceful. She trades her sister access to

Jacob for some of the mandrakes that Leah's son Reuben has collected; in ancient times, the cousin of the potato was believed to enhance fertility.

She's prone to a little drama: "Give me children, or I shall die!" she says to her husband.[2] And later, even as she names her first son, she's already asking for another.

She has an ambiguous relationship with God, as the womanist biblical scholar Wil Gafney points out. The text most often identifies God as Jacob's God, her husband's God, as if Rachel held this God at arm's length. Scripture records that God blesses her and remembers her. But she speaks about God only three times, making observations about divine favor. If she ever directly addressed God—if she ever prayed—we never learn about it. But Scripture does tell us that "God heeded her," opening her womb. "God is involved in Rachel's life in the most intimate way, granting her the desire of her heart," Gafney writes, "even though she does not turn to God for help."[3]

I find something profoundly liberating in Gafney's reading of Rachel and deeply moving in the biblical depiction of someone so vibrantly, unquestionably human.

Rachel dies giving birth to her second child, a son. With her last breath, she names the boy Ben-oni: "son of my sorrow." In what might be read as an ancient act of toxic positivity and enduring patriarchy—she was obviously all in her feelings, right?—Jacob disregards Rachel's voice and instead calls him Benjamin: "son of the right hand."[4]

There are so many entrancing weirdnesses in Rachel's story as it's recorded in Scripture. Susan Niditch, a scholar of the

Hebrew Scriptures, highlights Rachel's theft of her father's teraphim—the little objects that some versions translate as "household gods" and other scholars believe to be representations of venerated ancestors. Rachel hides the teraphim under the saddle of her camel, sits on said camel, and then claims she can't rise to greet her father because "the way of women is upon me." She uses a distinctly female power to control the situation, in a stunning instance of antipatriarchal direct action. Citing Rachel's "clever exploitation of that which makes her most markedly female," Niditch identifies this as a rare and unusual instance in which "covert woman's power . . . dominates man's overt authority."[5]

So much of Rachel's story happens off the page, from how she actually manages the tricky relationships with her sister-wives to what those quiet moments with Jacob were like. But I imagine that the shrewdness evident elsewhere in the text pervaded all her interactions.

When we're reminded that Jesus is the Good Shepherd, often people amplify the echo in the metaphor of David, the unlikely young shepherd who conquered a giant and started a kingdom. I like to think, too, of Rachel, the unlikely young shepherd who strategized with her entire body, loved with a passionate fury, and then gave her life for her child.

⁂

The bigger point here is that there are different ways to read a text, different angles from which to perceive it. It's like a gemstone that captures, catches, and reflects different light.

No facet can represent that gemstone in its entirety. It has to be turned and regarded from various directions for us to begin to glimpse the beauty of the whole.

The late French philosopher Jacques Derrida had a wonderful phrase, "impoverishment by univocality," that he deployed to call for a kind of reading (or listening) that seeks instead to amplify the richness of multiple perspectives. When we try to make a text univocal, reducing it to one voice, we fail to recognize the full possibility of what it can offer. To interpret a piece of writing with the goal of "getting to the point" is to fail to recognize the wealth within and beyond it, because it takes on new life and new layers when it's interpreted through the diverse lens of the many. To understand the Bible and its meaning as "clear" and "plain" is to diminish its relevance to peoples across time and space and to fail to recognize that the Bible is anything but univocal.

The same can be said of how we see, describe, and attribute action to God. We impose masks on God, choosing to emphasize particular perspectives and downplay others, lifting particular understandings while minimizing others. Some of these masks ended up written down in Scripture, while others are lost to memory; some are more literary in nature, while others can be seen as more historical. The literary masks of God—at least the ones that ended up in the Bible or in other religious writings—do have a historical dimension to them, for each bears witness to the way God has patiently accommodated people's fallen and culturally conditioned conceptions of the divine at a particular moment in history. But I say that these masks are primarily literary, not historical, because I refuse to believe that God engaged in or commanded the violence that some Old Testament authors ascribe to God.

All this might sound complicated, but it's not, not really. We all wear our own masks, which to varying degrees represent who we are as well as who we imagine ourselves to be as well as who we aspire to be. Even the more fictitious ones can tell us something. We can learn from what lurks in the shadows.

In *Life of the Beloved*, Henri Nouwen writes about the masks of the world—or, rather, about liberating yourself from them. "You have to keep unmasking the world about you for what it is: manipulative, controlling, power-hungry, and, in the long run, destructive," he writes. "The world tells you many lies about who you are, and you simply have to be realistic enough to remind yourself of this."[6]

The world tells us many lies about who God is too. And my hope in calling us to take care with how we read stories about God, about God's people, and about ourselves and our communities, is ultimately that we will not give those lies more power than they deserve, which is to say, not much power at all.

It seems too good to be true that God redeems all things, and yet this is the hope that has been written for us. No matter which angle I perceive this from, it just seems . . . good. Hard but good. Unbelievable but good. Weird but good.

To return to Tennyson:

> Oh, yet we trust that somehow good
> Will be the final end of ill,
> To pangs of nature, sins of will,
> Defects of doubt, and taints of blood;
>
> That nothing walks with aimless feet;
> That not one life shall be destroy'd,
> Or cast as rubbish to the void,
> When God hath made the pile complete.

# 11

# WILDERNESS

The path from unquestioning certainty to wholehearted vulnerability looks less like a wide, paved, flat boulevard than a winding, sometimes barely discernible track through steep hills and debris-strewn valleys. In other words, it looks a lot like a forbidding journey through the wilderness.

I've written before about the wilderness, which in Scripture is both a literal destination and a metaphorical trope. I like a little bit of controlled wilderness every now and then—a hike in the hills with my family, taken with the hope of a hot shower after a successful day out, or a (very) brief camping trip that comes with the promise of AC and cable TV at its conclusion. That is obviously not how the biblical or spiritual wilderness works.

Wilderness can be at once a place of refuge and a space of

disquietude. It can be where you both sigh in relief and feel your heart pounding nearly out of your chest as you approach the unknown. Jesus sought solitude in the wilderness—I tell myself that he was an introvert like I am, and I imagine him scampering over boulders just to get away from the insatiable crowds—but it was also where he was tempted. The wilderness can bring clear, constellation-filled night skies and the gentle, reassuring murmur of a stream making its way inexorably downhill. It might also mean a viper, unseen until too late, or the utter disappointment of brambles without berries.

Hagar has become one of my favorite heroes in Scripture in recent years. She is a woman of incredible valor. She is also a veteran of the wilderness; she finds herself there twice, or maybe three times, depending on how you want to define "wilderness."

Enslaved in her native Egypt, she ends up far from home, laboring in the household of Abram and Sarai. Forcibly impregnated in a quickly regretted scheme to give childless Abram an heir, she nurtures both the promise of her son and contempt for her slave mistress. Sarai has the audacity to be angry at Hagar's derision, exacting her fury on her husband as well as on Hagar. Sarai's behavior is as hideous as Hagar's is heroic, because then Hagar just leaves.

"Hagar becomes the first female in the Bible to liberate herself from oppressive power structures," the womanist scholar Delores Williams writes. "Though the law prescribes harsh punishment for run-away slaves, she takes the risk rather than endure more brutal treatment by Sarai."[1] Hagar makes herself vulnerable to unknown dangers rather than continue at the cruel hands of a bitter captor. She throws herself out of one wilderness—this foreign and oppressive household—straight into another.

The wilderness is where an angel of God finds Hagar—and not just anywhere in the wilderness but by a spring of water. It is on the one hand a troubling narrative, because the angel instructs Hagar to return to enslavement, and a comforting one, because the angel also promises blessing in the form of many descendants and says that God "has given heed to your affliction."[2]

She returns to the household of Abram and Sarai, though she disappears from the narrative while the couple are getting their names changed, dealing with the destruction of Sodom and Gomorrah, taking a trip, pretending to be siblings, and welcoming their son Isaac. Name aside, though, Sarah hasn't changed much; she can't stand it when she sees Isaac and Ishmael playing together, and she instructs her seemingly feckless husband to kick Hagar and Ishmael out.

"The matter was very distressing to Abraham on account of his son," Scripture tells us. The next line is interesting: "But God said to Abraham, 'Do not be distressed because of the boy and because of your slave woman.'"[3] There is no evidence that Abraham was ever distressed about Hagar, only about the boy. Is this some kind of divine shade being thrown at Abraham's patriarchy? Is this God saying, "Hmm . . . you might have left someone out in this situation"?

Regardless, the story tells us that God makes some promises, which makes Abraham feel better, so he packs Hagar and Ishmael a picnic lunch and sends them out into the wilderness. Here's some bread, here's some water—have a nice life! This is not a liberation; it is an abandonment.

The wilderness is where an angel of God finds Hagar again. She is weeping, not for her own sake but for the life of her child, whom she has cast under the cool shade of a bush. Then she has walked away, unable to bear the possibility that she might have to watch her son die of starvation or thirst.

On the ground and out of the safety of his mother's arms, the baby cries out too. God hears this heart-wrenching chorus— mother and child, both begging for some version of salvation. And a voice comes from heaven, saying, "Do not be afraid."[4] (This is only the second time in Scripture that these words have rushed down in divine blessing. The first was for Abram before he became Abraham, as he was about to leave his native land and make his own journey into the unknown.)

Then God opens Hagar's eyes to a well that she had not seen. As Williams observes, "God gave her new vision to see survival resources where she saw none before," the wilderness transforming into a place of provision.[5] And finally come words of benediction that any parent could appreciate: "God was with the boy."[6] Could any mother ask for anything more?

Many of my childhood family vacations were spent visiting historic sites and national parks—"managed" wilderness held in trust for the people of the United States. And since we stayed close-ish to home, that meant lots of trips to the Great Smoky Mountains. As Amanda and I got older, we ventured farther afield. In Massachusetts, my dad and I visited Walden Pond, hoping for some inspiration from the lingering spirit of Henry David Thoreau. (It ended up being more irritation, at the crowds of swimmers, the lifeguards, and the incessant whistles at the once-peaceful pond.) We went to the Grand Tetons and to Yellowstone, to the Badlands and to the Rocky Mountains.

When I was sixteen, my parents loaded my sister and me into our Plymouth Voyager minivan and we embarked on an epic road trip through ten states and one Canadian province. We stopped in Hannibal, Missouri, where I got to see the desk where Mark Twain wrote; Fairfield, Iowa (Hi, Uncle Ray and Aunt Laurel!); Colorado Springs, Colorado (Hi, Aunt Diane and Uncle Dave!); and the gorgeous scenery around Lake Louise, in Alberta, where we watched, from the safety of the van, a black bear tearing through a fallen tree. Really, though, this trip ended up being about one place for me, a wilderness that imprinted itself on my heart: Glacier National Park in Montana.

It's hard to put into words exactly what so entranced me about Glacier, just as it's hard to pinpoint the mechanics of love. Was it the friendly mountain goat that greeted Amanda and me in the parking lot of a visitor center or the moose and her calves we met behind the Swiftcurrent Motor Inn? The drip, drip, drip of adrenaline as we hiked the trails, constantly on the lookout for bears? Or maybe it was the wildflower carpet atop Logan Pass: yellow from the glacier lily and the blueleaf cinquefoil, crimson from the red monkeyflower and the aptly named firewheel, purple from the alpine willowweed and the mountain laurel—colors that might be messy and garish in someone's living room but, scattered across meadows under the wide ceiling of the Montana sky, were spectacular.

When Dan and I decided to take a trip to mark our tenth wedding anniversary, I knew I wanted to go back to Glacier, and not just to Glacier but to the Many Glacier Hotel. This lodge, where I stayed for just one night with my parents and Amanda, sits on the shore of Swiftcurrent Lake, a mile-long, snowmelt-filled gash. Mountains ring the water, as if to use the still surface as a mirror in which to admire themselves.

Glacier National Park is moving. My favorite spot in the entire world is the back deck of the Many Glacier Hotel. To sit there, a warm mug of coffee in hand, is to encounter the paradox of intimate majesty. The vista both stirs my heart and calms my soul.

But I also mean "moving" in another way: it's actually moving. Rocks, ice, and gravity have worked in concert for thousands upon thousands of years to carve these valleys and shape these peaks. Some two dozen glaciers still do their slow and steady work. The landscape changes constantly. In the alpine tundra above the tree line, snow piles up for more than half the year, and when it finally loses its battle against the warming seasons and reveals what's beneath, hardy perennials take furious advantage of their moment in the sun. A few plants show themselves even more rarely; the rock harlequin, for instance, doesn't typically flower except in the year or two after a fire.

Maybe the multidimensional reality of a place like Glacier can help us understand the complexity of the imagery of Scripture and even of our faith. For those of us taught to fear fire and brimstone as punishment, perhaps it's instructive that sometimes fire can mean needed warmth on a cold night, that sometimes fire cleanses and clarifies, that sometimes fire is even a liberating force that cracks open the seeds of new life that would otherwise remain dormant, waiting for freedom.

How is it that a mountain goat can find such steady footing on these vertiginous slopes? What map does it read that shows it the way home? Maybe the wilderness seems as forbidding as it does just because we don't have the muscle memory to navigate or the skills to climb and sense.

What does a western hemlock, that grand conifer that can live more than half a millennium, think when a youngster like me comes along? Chanterelle mushrooms got to know this tree, finding ample places to grow at its feet. Native Americans got to know this tree too. They understood that its bark was edible and a good base for cakes, and that its young needles could be brewed into a tea rich in vitamin C. The Coastal Salish peoples of what is now Canada built shelters for menstruating women using western hemlock branches, and this species was said to have particularly feminine energy.

What if the "problem" with the wilderness isn't a problem with the wilderness at all but rather with us, with our lack of knowledge, and with our truncated imagination? The wilderness reminds us that things aren't usually as simple or one-dimensional as they seem. Our stereotypes of such spaces imagine them as places of exile, spaces of lifelessness. That would be a surprise to the creatures that call it home.

Perhaps the real struggle is ours. We don't like not knowing. Indeed, we fear it.

Sometimes wilderness comes to us even when we don't want it. In her book *Glory Happening*, my friend Kaitlin Curtice meditates on a Christmas flood that hit the Ozarks, a space of mountains and valleys that her people had once known as home. What had been a place of idyllic calm was transformed, and as she and her family drove through this deluged landscape, everything seemed new. "Trees were only showing their top halves, leafless and cold," Kaitlin writes. "The flood covered everything—rivers risen almost to bridges, and whole highway sections closed."[7]

A flood can bring immense destruction; we know that from contemporary headlines as well as from ancient Scripture. What I appreciate about Kaitlin's reflection, though, is that she reminds us this isn't the only story. "A flood is a funny thing," she continues. "For all the grief that can come with it, it also brings a deep and full cleansing, wiping everything away to start again—new spaces, new grasses, spreading seeds, and digging up roots. Maybe the trees said, 'Finally, I can drink my fill, my roots have been thirsty for so long.' And maybe the grass whispered, 'In the spring I will be greener than ever, because this water has given me new life.'"[8]

Maybe.

Maybe.

Maybe.

Maybe the call of the wilderness is to ask us to think more deeply, more broadly, more adventurously, more boldly, about the maybes.

Whenever Scripture takes us into the wilderness, it is usually not the barren wasteland that it at first seems. Over and over, God's people are led to springs that flow with water, and somehow there is enough sustenance that shepherds can graze their livestock there. All manner of life—snakes and scorpions, broom trees and owls, wild donkeys and ostriches—finds home amidst the untamed terrain, and if the wilderness howls, it is because it is alive with jackals. Even the scapegoat finds freedom there—humility and salvation.

Do we call it wild because we haven't figured out how to conquer it? Do we find it forbidding not because it is forbidden but because it's simply foreign?

Maybe one of the lessons is that the wilderness is a place where we can't rely on the familiar, which can seem like a hardship but might also be an invitation—an invitation into the reality of our existence, an invitation into the truth of our vulnerability.

After the Israelites had survived their long journey through the wilderness, they were reminded that it was the place "where you saw how the Lord your God carried you," Deuteronomy says, "just as one carries a child."[9]

Maybe that can be true for us too.

## 12

# GOD HAS MADE A
# HOME WITH US

I still struggle many days to believe that God loves me just as I am, not as I could be. Who doesn't? "The glorious message of Scripture is that we do not have to be perfect for our Maker to love us," Madeleine L'Engle wrote. "All through the great stories, heavenly love is lavished on visibly imperfect people."[1]

L'Engle cited Jacob, the son of Isaac and Rebekah, who lied his way to a blessing. It's a complicated story, and Jacob a complicated character. For centuries, rabbis have tussled with this story, turning it this way and that to fill in the blanks that the text itself leaves. In L'Engle's reading, "Scripture asks us to look at Jacob as he really is, to look at ourselves as we really are, and then realize that this is who God loves."[2]

Pause here and take a deep breath with me, because I am totally fine with looking at Jacob as he really is. But looking at myself? As I really am? Not so much. That is in some ways its own kind of personal wilderness, when I'd prefer to remain within the comforts of the suburban home of my cushy spirituality.

"God did not love Jacob because he was a cheat, but because he was Jacob," L'Engle continued. "God loves us in our complex *is*ness, and when we get stuck on the totally virtuous and morally perfect person we will never be, we are unable to accept this unqualified love, or to love other people in their rich complexity."[3]

In other words, what if God's love were right there for us this whole time? But rather than recognizing what has been prepared for us, rather than falling wholeheartedly into what is already ours, we spend so much of our time and energy trying to earn it. We act as if we can perform our way to absolution of our sins. We think we need to wow the Almighty into wanting our company. We believe we can dazzle God into loving us.

Could God really be so gullible? Is the Divine so easily impressed?

I've come to believe that the only thing we're actually accomplishing is exhausting ourselves. In doing so, we distract ourselves from the beautiful truth and the gorgeous reality: God already loves us.

For all that's wrong with white American evangelicalism, I'm thankful to have grown up in a church tradition that emphasized the importance of nurturing a "personal relationship" with God. From an early age, I had a deep and active prayer life, which meant that I was comfortable shooting the breeze with Jesus about whatever happened to be on my mind: my friends, my sins, my hopes, my questions, my fears, my obsession with that boy . . . Jesus heard it all.

Sometimes in the churches of my childhood, though, it seemed one way people tried to dazzle God was through prayer. More was more—more words, more reminders to God of God's own greatness, more repetitions of the phrase "Father God." This kind of prayer seemed like performance, and as I've grown older, I've had to ask: Performance for whom? If we really believe that God can see past our facades, what is the point of this kind of prayer?

The Bible scholar Ellen Davis, who teaches at Duke Divinity School, indicts the superficial way in which many people pray, offering up the Psalms as examples of precisely the opposite. The Psalms, she explains, are about "speaking our mind honestly and fully before God."[4]

Yet we tend to remember the gentle psalms, which send us pastoral scenes and postcards of still waters, as well as the celebratory ones, resplendent with shouts of acclamation and rhapsodic verse. At times it can feel as if the various psalmists were themselves vying for some ancient Most Godly Poetry prize. For those of us who have harbored doubt and uncertainty in our hearts, these psalms can feel like a rebuke, as if we were not holy enough to ward off our fears.

We forget about Psalm 44, which feels accusatory and even rude in the way it tries to instigate a divine guilt trip: "In God we have boasted continually," the psalmist cries, "Yet you have rejected us . . . Rouse yourself! Why do you sleep, O Lord? . . . Awake!"[5]

We forget about Psalm 58, which even the most charitable reader couldn't exactly take as gentle or kind. This one contains graphic and harsh prayers: that God might treat the psalmist's enemies like a "snail that dissolves into slime" and that God might bring upon them pain like a woman's "untimely birth that never sees the sun"—one that's especially brutal to read as someone who has experienced miscarriage.[6]

We forget about Psalm 88, which blames God for putting the psalmist "in the depths of the Pit" and asserts that God is the cruelest kind of social engineer: "You have caused my companions to shun me; you have made me a thing of horror to them."[7] This is also the one that, unlike the others, ends not in rapturous praise but rather in utter despair.

We might be instinctively turned off by some of the content or tone of the Psalms. There's a small part of me that also feels righteously indignant: *I've* never talked to God like that. *I've* never asked God to slay my enemies, except in the most metaphorical of ways. But there's also something significant about the fact that what concerned these authors, the gory and real details of their cultural and social locations, made it into Scripture. There's an invitation here that is compelling.

Reading Davis, I got to feeling as if these psalms were a kind of spiritual turpentine, dissolving the layers of paint that mask the truth of the human condition, paint that was chipping away anyway. "These biblical prayers expose the hollow sentimentality that often masquerades as prayer, the dangerous falsity of things we have heard—and maybe even thought ourselves—about how we ought to think and talk when God is around," she writes. "Things like this: *God does not have any use for our anger*; we must have already forgiven our enemy before God will listen to our prayer."[8]

Davis pushes back hard against not only the idea that we can't express our anger, righteous or not, *to* God but also even the notion that we can't or shouldn't be angry *at* God. She sees such prohibitive thinking as a harmful tool that has prevented us from having a richer prayer life, because we're still trying to sculpt artificially beautiful conversations with God. But if it's true that there can be no real intimacy without vulnerability, and if that describes our relationships with other human beings, how much more must it be true of the One we call God?

God's invitation into wholeheartedness means recognizing that God cares about the desires of my heart, even if that heart isn't perfect. It means understanding that God is concerned about the things that concern me. It means coming to terms, in yet another way, with the truth that God loves me.

One of my favorite prayers in the Bible is Mary's Magnificat.

The Magnificat is the longest speech by a woman in the

New Testament. It's a striking prayer in that Mary doesn't really ask for anything. This contrasts with how many of us typically pray, which more resembles an appointment with a personal shopper (I'm imagining—I've never had a personal shopper) than a conversation with the Creator of the universe.

While we typically like to paint Mary in the softer hues—her robes clean and bright, her hair combed and covered, her body poised in prayerful and serene surrender—this young woman was a fierce one, full of strength and fury. When she accepts the dangerous charge before her (every birth in those days was a risky one), she does not recite a demure maternal blessing or whisper a gentle word to heaven. Instead, she offers a prayer that doubles as prophecy, giving powerful voice to the paradoxical already-and-not-yet of God:

> "My soul magnifies the Lord,
> and my spirit rejoices in God my Savior,
> for he has looked with favor on the lowliness of his
>     servant.
> Surely, from now on all generations will call me
>     blessed;
> for the Mighty One has done great things for me,
> and holy is his name.
> His mercy is for those who fear him
> from generation to generation.
> He has shown strength with his arm;
> he has scattered the proud in the thoughts of their
>     hearts.
> He has brought down the powerful from their thrones,

and lifted up the lowly;
he has filled the hungry with good things,
and sent the rich away empty.
He has helped his servant Israel,
in remembrance of his mercy,
according to the promise he made to our ancestors,
to Abraham and to his descendants forever."[9]

When the Magnificat is sung in a warm, candlelit church at Advent, it can be easy to feel these words rounded and softened. It can lull us into imagining them as comforting, nonspecific, and even symbolic. But there are times when that hasn't felt right at all—and I wonder whether that sort of gauzy sentimentality might even be a misreading of this prayer, which echoes the most bracing psalms with its boldness and its candor.

In some seasons, it has felt more appropriate to imagine Mary's Magnificat being shouted, not sung.

In the Michelin-starred restaurants and on the floors of stock exchanges . . .

"He has filled the hungry with good things, and sent the rich away empty!"

In the corridors of the West Wing and the Capitol . . .

"He has brought down the powerful from their thrones, and lifted up the lowly!"

In the streets of Charlottesville and Hong Kong, Moscow and Mandalay . . .

"He has shown strength with his arm; he has scattered the proud in the thoughts of their hearts!"

Among women who have survived assault, harassment, and rape only to be publicly maligned by their powerful abusers . . .

"He has looked with favor on the lowliness of his servant! Surely, from now on all generations will call me blessed!"

Among the poor, the refugees, the victims of gun violence, and the faithful ministers of the Gospel who are speaking with courage against the false religions of nationalism and white supremacy . . .

"His mercy is for those who fear him from generation to generation!"

In the Magnificat, Mary isn't merely making a birth announcement. This prayer is definitely not the ancient Palestinian equivalent of a gender reveal party. Her words are not the scriptural equivalent of cutting a buttercream cake that turns out to have bright blue frosting inside. Instead, Mary's holy soliloquy seems breathtaking in its bravado: she declares the inauguration of a new kingdom, one that stands in stark contrast to every other regime—past, present, and future—that relies on violence and exploitation to achieve "greatness."

In some ancient liturgical volumes, the Magnificat was called by another name: the *Evangelium Mariae*, the Gospel of Mary. This seems right, because there is so much good news in her prayer. Mary proclaims that God has indeed chosen sides. And it's not with the powerful but with the humble. It's not with the rich but with the poor. It's not with the occupying force but with people who are occupied and oppressed, disregarded and disempowered. It's not with vain, narcissistic kings but with an unwed, unbelieved teenage girl entrusted with the holy task of birthing, nursing, and nurturing God.

In her defiant prayer, Mary—a dark-skinned woman who will become a refugee, a member of a religious minority in a colonized land—names the reality of the coming Incarnation: God is with us. And if God is with us, who can stand against us?

Sometimes I forget this, though. Instead, I wallow with the angst of the prophets and the restlessness of the psalmists. "How long, O Lord?" they asked, and I ask. "Will you hide your face forever?"

Sometimes I forget to summon Mary's courageous spirit.

Sometimes I forget her acknowledgments not of what she is doing but of what God has already done.

Sometimes I forget that this remarkable woman prayed a prayer that didn't make any requests. Instead, she simply called it like she saw it, proclaiming in ridiculously bold present tense that the great reversal had already arrived. Shouldn't we echo such holy audacity?:

> The powerful have been humbled.
> The vulnerable have been lifted up.
> God has made a home among the people.
> God has made a home with us, in all our beautiful
>     complexity and in all our magnificent mess.

Notice that Mary does not shy away from naming sin. Sin is real, reluctant as we may be to speak of it, except in the most general terms when it comes to ourselves or in smug specificity when it comes to others. Sin separates us from God. And sin damages our relationships with one another.

In ancient Greek, one of the meanings of the root of the word "demon" is "to throw apart." In other words, anything that disintegrates us, anything that divides us, anything that destroys our wholeness, is demonic. I see the ways in which I have tried to tear myself to pieces, parsing what's good and what's bad, what's worthwhile and what's not. So perhaps there's some unwitting truth to all the detractors who have told me on Twitter that I'm demonic.

One of the biggest obstacles in my adult prayer life has been thinking that the stuff I care about is so trivial and stupid that God couldn't possibly care about it, which is its own form of slander against a God who repeatedly shows up, a God who knows all and sees all. There are, for instance, the (many) times that I've gotten so worked up about writing deadlines that I've lost all perspective.

A few years ago, not long after my son was born, I turned in a draft to my editor that I was convinced was an abomination unto the Lord. It was the first book I'd tried to write while parenting. At one point, as my deadline neared, things got so bad that we flew my mother-in-law down from New Jersey to help with childcare. It totally shattered her romantic notions of the writing life, and she might have said to me more than once: "Don't let the baby see you crying."

After submitting that tearstained, coffee-fueled draft, I flew to Michigan to teach a writing workshop. As I prepared to share with the gathered students all the collected wisdom gleaned from my perfect writer's life, I got a text message from my husband, Dan, who had been making the bed. He had found, on my side amid the sheets, he said, "a commentary on Luke and a couple of Cheez-Its."

What if God cares about my messy writing life and my overconsumption of coffee, my stray Cheez-Its and my choice of Gospel commentary, simply because God cares about me? What if it isn't trivial and stupid to God because it isn't trivial and stupid to me?

In that way, prayer can be a rebuke of what's demonic and an invitation to return to wholeness. And if it is indeed a call to wholeness, it can't just be within me; it also must be between me and those around me.

I will declare to you all day long that the purpose of a child of God is to love indiscriminately and unconditionally, just as God has loved us. This is what we were made to do and this is who we were made to be. But . . .

There's a beautiful and terrible passage in Frederick Buechner's *Whistling in the Dark* that reminds me of the difficulty of achieving this purpose, especially when we remember Jesus's radical call for us to love our enemies and pray for those who persecute us. How? What exactly is prayer supposed to do when it comes to our feelings about those we struggle to love?

What Buechner describes is a kind of attentive compassion, a sort of meditative reframing that happens in the process of surrendering your feelings about your enemy to the God who made your enemy and loves your enemy too. "You see the lines in their faces and the way they walk when they're tired. You see who their husbands and wives are, maybe. You see where they're vulnerable. You see where they're scared," he writes.

"Seeing what is hateful about them, you may catch a glimpse also of where the hatefulness comes from. Seeing the hurt they cause you, you may see also the hurt they cause themselves."[10]

Buechner writes with wondrous, inspiring clarity about the human condition and our capacity to love. "You're still light-years away from loving them, to be sure, but at least you see how they are human even as you are human, and that is at least a step in the right direction," he continues. "It's possible that you may even get to where you can pray for them a little, if only that God forgive them because you yourself can't, but any prayer for them at all is a major breakthrough."[11]

Prayer, then, even a momentary one that lasts no longer than the flutter of a butterfly's wings, nudges us just a little bit closer to God, wholeness, and love, and it pushes us just a little bit further from what's unholy, demonic, and hateful. I like to think of prayer—especially as modeled by the Psalms—as a way that God holds space for the things that weigh us down and trouble us as well as the things that bemuse us and confound us. Prayer is a sacred space in which God invites us just to be—to be imperfect, to be messy, to be a ball of conflicting emotions, to be all of who we are this side of heaven.

To return to Ellen Davis's depiction of the Psalms, she writes that these prayers "give us words for all the moods in which we come before God: adoration, exultation, gratitude; but also rage, despair, fear—those feelings which, as 'saints,' we feel required to deny."[12] But what good is sainthood if it's only half human? What point is there to being with God if we can only do so while partially masked?

It isn't, and there isn't, and the good news of the Psalms

is that they contain God's invitation to wholehearted expression of where we are—and who we are. In one of my favorite passages of Davis's *Getting Involved with God*, she meditates on Psalm 102, a particularly vivid lament psalm written as a prayer of an oppressed person, when weak and pouring out grief to God.

> For I eat ashes like bread,
> and mingle tears with my drink,
> because of your indignation and anger;
> for you have lifted me up and thrown me aside.
> My days are like an evening shadow;
> I wither away like grass.[13]

I get this: for the past few years, my regular cocktail has been a shot of my own tears stirred with a shot of Jack Daniel's, a drink I call America Under Forty-Five. But maybe praying this psalm, or some version of it, would be a healthier option. This psalm would have provided to ancient worshippers the balm that only clear-eyed examination of one's situation could. "This psalm does for them what promises of long life and abundance could not do," Davis writes. "It locates their reality on the map of faith."[14]

This is one of the things I've been missing in many contemporary articulations of Christianity—a raw, unadorned expression of how much things can truly suck. There is no judgment, at least not as we think of it. There is no condemnation of the psalmist's wallowing, no admonition that he ought to be something other than what he is or feel something other than what he feels. There is no patronizing suggestion that this is all part of God's plan.

In the context of many of our modern churches, Psalm 102 offers a countercultural cry. This is not what we customarily consider to be appropriate expression on the Lord's Day. This is not how we're taught to talk to God. This is not how we typically show up in worship, unless you enjoy that mid-service move seemingly patented by at least one stern old lady in every congregation—you know the slow turn in the pew up front, followed by that killer glare just over the tops of her glasses.

But the God of our cultural imaginations isn't the God of Scripture. The God of Scripture is the God who went to weddings, grilled fish on the beach with his friends, and wept at a loved one's death. And the invitation here is not to pontificate about salvation or write a treatise about redemption; it's to pray. It's to present yourself honestly to the God who saw a man who scraped his open sores with shards of pottery, the God who told us a story about a father throwing a fatted calf on the fire to celebrate the return of a long-lost son, the God who himself quoted one of those ancient prayers to wonder whether he had been forsaken.

It's all right there in Scripture—and there it has been for thousands of years, sung together in worship.

At least in Psalm 102 there is a turn toward hope, even if it might seem to some who pray this prayer as a cry of fantasy: "He will regard the prayer of the destitute, and will not despise their prayer."[15]

Often we won't have our own words to describe the full

expanse of our spiritual landscape, bleak and windswept as it might feel. But we have the Psalms, and the Psalms help me remember why I can still call this faith my own: it makes room for complexity and does not attempt to deny life's convolutions. "As we take the Psalms on our lips one by one, we eventually claim each of those experiences and feelings as our own," Davis continues, "and thus we enter fully into the life of all those who call themselves Israel."[16]

"With my whole heart, I cry," Psalm 119:145 says; "answer me, O Lord." And I echo the psalmist:

> With my whole heart, I cry out to you, God.
> With all my sadness.
> With all my anger.
> With all my fear that I have not done enough and therefore am not enough.
> With all my residual shame about my childhood eczema.
> With all my longing to be seen for who I am—and who I want to be.
> With all my respect and honor for my parents.
> With all my indignation at leaders who misuse their power.
> With all my absurd delight at *30 Rock*.
> With all my frustration at gun policies that don't change.
> With all my annoyance at the people who accuse me of "getting political" and who say they liked me better when I wasn't.

With all my doubts that praying does anything.

With all my praise for the gift of sisterhood, for the gift of Amanda.

With all my fury at those who subjugate others because of their gender, their sexuality, their ethnicity, or their nationality.

With all my mixed feelings about Twitter.

With all my love for Dan, for my son, and for my daughter.

With all my confused emotions about *PAW Patrol*.

With all my complicated gratitude for the churches of my upbringing and for white American evangelicalism.

With all my disgust for the arrogance of American exceptionalism.

With all my pettiness about poorly written biographies of Dietrich Bonhoeffer.

With all my affectionate snark as expressed in text messages to my friends.

With all my worries that I might have gotten it all wrong.

With all my thanks for dark chocolate and Cheez-Its.

With all my concerns about which aspects of Scripture I might have misunderstood or misread.

With all my hope for the healing of the world.

With my whole heart, I cry.

That's all I can do. Now answer me, O Lord, and let me rest in your goodness, for you have made a home with us.

# 13

# LOVING OUR ENEMIES

The last Why Christian? conference was held at Grace Cathedral, which sits atop Nob Hill in San Francisco. Nadia Bolz-Weber, nine other men and women, and I offered our testimonies, giving twenty-minute talks about why we're still Christians.

The altar behind us had its own story to tell. The Grace Cathedral altar is hewn of granite from the Sierra Nevada and redwood. It was long believed to be a California redwood, because it came from a lumberyard in Northern California. But this was just conjecture and hearsay, and you know how rumor can morph into truth in church.

A few years ago, the church invited a dendrochronologist to visit, to see whether she could decipher anything more definite about the origins of the tree from which that altar was crafted. It's amazing what stories are etched into a piece of timber. Counting the rings helps tell us how old a tree was when it was felled. The distances between those rings provides a record of what was happening in that tree's native forest in any given year, whether it was flood or drought or fire. By comparing an individual tree's ingrained testimony against those of other trees, we can also get some indication of that tree's geographic origins.

There are three distinct species of redwood, and a careful study of the altar at Grace Cathedral confirmed that this was indeed a coast redwood. Its Latin name, *Sequoia sempervirens*, speaks of this species' longevity; *sempervirens* means "living forever." That's only a slight exaggeration: coast redwoods can live for more than two thousand years, which means today's oldest living redwoods were youngsters when Jesus walked the earth.

The scientist was able to confirm that this redwood dated to the late sixteenth or early seventeenth century. And the patterns left in the tree rings were clear enough to say that this tree came from Northern California's forests, up the coast from San Francisco.

Coast redwoods can grow as tall as 350 feet, their trunks more than 20 feet in diameter, and the crowns of these gentle giants as wide as 100 feet. Those crowns contain countless jewels—vast and vibrant communities virtually invisible to the creatures far below on the forest floor. Nestled in the branches are birds and worms and salamanders. Ferns and mosses flourish up there, soaking up the fog that sweeps in off the Pacific, as do huckleberry bushes, whose brambles entwine with the ferns and mosses, all of them drawing nutrients from the decaying leaf litter dropped from branches even higher up.

Beneath the soil, there's another, significant subterranean story: for a tree so tall and grand, the roots of the coast redwood run remarkably shallow. Most redwoods have roots that go no farther than 5 or 10 feet deep. Instead, they roam far and wide, interlacing with the root networks of their neighbors. When storms roll in from the Pacific Ocean—one memorable system in 1962 produced gusts of up to 170 miles per hour—those neighbors hold on to one another for dear life, drawing stability from community and safety in numbers.

And then one more (when is David Attenborough going to do a series on these trees?): even after a majestic redwood falls, whether by human hand or in a devastating fire, death might not be the end of its story. From the roots of that one tree, new saplings can sprout. Often they do so in a stand encircling the ancestor, as if to testify to the one who came before. "For there is hope for a tree," the Book of Job says, "if it is cut down, that it will sprout again, and that its shoots will not cease. Though its root grows old in the earth, and its stump dies in the ground, yet at the scent of water it will bud and put forth branches like a young plant."[1]

The great French philosopher Simone Weil wrote, "To be rooted is perhaps the most important and least recognized need of the human soul."[2] The redwoods help remind me just why that is.

As much as I'd like to say that I don't need anyone else, that I can exist independently and autonomously, that would be a lie. It's a Christian commonplace to say that God created us for relationship, that we were made for community. And though we might consistently fail to live out that call, it remains a commonplace because it's true.

It bears remembering that much of the New Testament was written not to individuals but to congregations, to little families of faith gathered around tables, breaking bread together and pouring wine together and hearing Scripture read together. When Paul wrote to the Roman believers, he hadn't even met them. They could not hear his voice through the words that were read out loud to them. And the only way through that thicket of theological discourse was together.

Most of the Hebrew Bible is still read as it has been for centuries, in worship in synagogues around the world. The ancient stories, the timeless psalms—these were all meant to be experienced in the companionship of other struggling, straining souls and alongside other fragile, aching bodies, not alone and not in isolation. "It is only in the reading and the rereading which each community does together that the Bible becomes a timeless text, the Word of God," the rabbi Burton Visotzky writes. "If and when that happens, the Bible ceases to be just another book, gathering dust on the shelf. In a community of readers a conversation takes place. The give and take of interpretation creates an extra voice in the room, the sound of Reading the Book."[3]

I might go even further and assert that we weren't made just for community—we were made for *communities*. If it's true, as

Visotzky argues, that the give and take of interpretation creates an extra voice in the room, it's also worth asking: Who
doesn't happen to be in any given room? Who hasn't been welcomed? Who is standing just outside the door, afraid to come
in? Who might not have even made it out of the parking lot?
Who couldn't even imagine doing a drive-by?

In recent years, I've learned so much about God, about
God's love, about the difficult journey of risk and love, from
those who never would or could have shown up, at least not
openly or willingly or fully, in the churches of my childhood:
people of color, LGBTQ+ people, atheists and agnostics, disabled and neurodivergent folks, immigrants and refugees. I've
encountered their voices and found their wisdom through social media and in the pages of books.

This attitude stands in stark contrast to the winner-take-
all posture in many fundamentalist Christian communities,
including the one I grew up in, which positions the solitary
reader, the individual of faith, with her personal relationship
with Jesus Christ, as the objective arbiter of truth. That person's interpretation of the text is final and exclusive. That
person's understanding of God is the be-all and end-all. The
refrain, as I remember it, goes something like this: "The Bible
said it, I believe it, that settles it." That's not exactly the sort
of gentle and loving conversation starter that brings people
together—or even into the room.

Conservatives, of course, have no monopoly on that fundamentalist mindset. On the progressive end of things, you hear
a similar refrain: "Science said it, I believe it, that settles it." Or
maybe "Rachel Maddow said it, I believe it, that settles it."

Or maybe "Barack Obama said it, I believe it, that settles it." Or maybe "Some rando on Twitter tweeted it, I agree with it, that settles it." That kind of fundamentalism, too, fails to acknowledge the dynamism of science, the fallibility of a human being, and the severe nuance deficit of social media.

One of my favorite quotes from the theologian James Cone reminds us that stories are relational and that there are multiple layers of relationship involved. "Every people has a story to tell, something to say to themselves, their children, and to the world about how they think and live, as they determine and affirm their reason for being," he wrote. "The story both expresses and participates in the miracle of moving from nothing to something, from nonbeing to being." For a story to matter, it must not only be told; it must also be heard—and in the hearing, there's an invitation. "As I listen to other stories," Cone continues, "I am invited to move out of the subjectivity of my own story into another realm of thinking and acting. The same is true for others when I tell my story."[4]

The challenge and call for us—no matter our community, no matter our *communities*—is to be faithful hearers and curious recipients, even and perhaps especially of stories that differ from our own.

We might all be weirdos, so it's not too hard to imagine how to love the oddball in your life or in your congregation. But then there's the difficult matter of one's enemies and Jesus's infuriating suggestion that we love them.

I have a nemesis. No, I won't name the person. Suffice it to say, they don't inspire the holiest reactions from me.

A meme-able quote has floated around for some years now that's been attributed to Buddhist thinkers and Christian ones, secular activists and religious figures: "An enemy is someone whose story you have not heard." Whoever said it, these words have the ring of truth but also an echo of error. Listening is not a panacea. Hearing another person's story is not an inevitable bridge across the gulf that might divide you, nor is it an express pass to friendship. If I hear the story of someone whose convictions include white supremacy and male superiority and who believes that I have no right to preach or publish, I've heard a story and maybe sacrificed some time, but it doesn't automatically mean I've expanded in my love for him.

While I'm a big believer in the power of stories to build relationship and to tear down walls, I also think loving our enemies requires more—including a better definition of what an enemy is.

Some, maybe even many, enemies are generalized, avatars for issues far bigger than themselves.

I remember how I immediately reacted when I learned that Osama bin Laden had been killed: like so many other people, I jumped on Twitter. Mike Huckabee wrote, "Welcome to hell,"[5] and Rob Bell fans declared, "Love wins." All different kinds of Christians were quoting all different kinds of Bible verses, and all different kinds of armchair pundits were offering all different kinds of poorly informed but incredibly confident commentary about what this would mean for the future of Al-Qaeda and the world.

Fortunately, I had the rare restraint that day not to tweet immediately. When I finally did, here's what I wrote: "Trying to keep in mind that how I respond to the death of my enemies says as much about me as it does about my enemies."[6] I still believe that. We cannot learn a lot about ourselves or one another by paying attention to how we respond to the death of a symbolic enemy.

The online back-and-forth, among Christians in the United States at least, had little to do with Osama bin Laden himself and everything to do with conflicting theological positions, competing agendas, and sensitive personality differences. Some of the deepest divides within Christendom regarding war, peace, politics, biblical interpretation, eschatology, and missiology surfaced in the aftermath of his death, and pronouncements regarding those divides said less about an enemy halfway around the world than they did about the ones within our own extended family of faith.

Other enemies hold such power over and within us because of their particular relationships to us.

This might be your playground bully—or the ghost of that bully, who continues to haunt you and taunt you years after you stopped having recess every day.

This might be an adversary at work, who snipes at you in ways you can't understand, or someone who used to be a friend, who knows you well enough to jab you in your most tender places, or someone who sometimes is a friend—the classic frenemy.

This might be a relative, who, for reasons known or unknown, just gives you the hardest time and doesn't seem to see, hear, or understand you.

This might also be you yourself, because sometimes we are our own worst enemies.

I am my own worst enemy when I wrap myself in the familiar but tattered blanket of my long-standing fears and insecurities, seeking comfort in the known rather than braving the elements of the unknown.

I am my own worst enemy when I rationalize my bad behavior and ignore the call to the good.

I am my own worst enemy when I fixate on the ugliest part of my personality without putting it into the context of the whole. Our most vitriolic critic can be that loathsome voice that shouts at us from within, and there's no way to escape it because how do you get away from yourself?

I am my own worst enemy when I isolate myself from the rest of humanity and convince myself that nobody else could possibly understand.

I am my own worst enemy when I justify my own sin.

I am my own worst enemy when I deny my own belovedness.

I am my own worst enemy when I call ugly what God has made beautiful and when I deem lovely what God has said is wrong, or when I take the ugly but untrue things that others have said and I believe them and nurture them and give them more influence than they deserve.

And starting with that acknowledgment that I can be my own worst enemy, perhaps I can begin to imagine how loving my enemies might look. Can we not only hear the enemy's story but also begin to write a different one—one that points toward God's shalom?

The writer and pastor Osheta Moore has explored the

concept of shalom extensively. It's a familiar Hebrew word, and it means "peace," but not necessarily peace as we typically understand it. It's not a false peace, like the grudging quiet that exists after two kids have stopped fighting and the adults have extracted muttered apologies. Instead, shalom is rooted in wholeness; indeed, that's the root of the Hebrew word. This peace points toward what Moore calls "God's dream for the world as it should be." This peace moves toward human flourishing. This peace "is what happens when the love of God pulls us out and says, I see you, you are beloved, and you are enough. And we are made whole," Moore said at the first Evolving Faith conference in 2018. "And then we turn around and make the world whole. . . . When we live into shalom, we are creating goodness all around us."[7]

Shalom pushes back against the idea that we are independent and recognizes that we are actually interdependent. "In the Hebraic view, shalom brings the binary mind together, integrating the left brain modality of thinking (linear) and the right brain modality (intuitive)," Rabbi David Zaslow writes. He notes that, in Hebrew, one says "shalom" as an initial greeting and one also says "shalom" as a form of farewell. "What is more opposite than coming and going? Hello and goodbye?" Zaslow continues, "Shalom is the most radical union of opposites imaginable. Shalom brings together people who disagree with each other so that each will listen deeply to the 'other' side. It is the people you do not agree with who have the greatest gift for you—the gift of the potential for wholeness."[8]

Which sounds wonderful in principle, but still, there's something deep within me that resists being brought together with those whom I find despicable—or who find me and what I believe to be the same. It's annoying. It's frustrating. Where do I even start, especially when I don't want to?

I've really been inspired by Shane Claiborne and The Simple Way's ongoing efforts to bring Isaiah 2 to life. That is the chapter that contains Isaiah's stirring prophecy of the coming of God's justice, a time in which people "shall beat their swords into plowshares, and their spears into pruning hooks."[9] Claiborne and his collaborators have traveled the country, turning guns into farming equipment.

Their example encouraged me to consider learning a new skill, one that would allow me to turn something ugly into something beautiful. Some years ago, I chose to do that as a Lenten practice. Whether it's turning an AK-47 into a rake, an old tire into a flower bed, or trash into a work of art, there is something profoundly fitting about struggling through the creative process with the goal of finishing something new by Easter to provide a tangible, hands-on experience in discipline, resurrection, and restoration.

As I prayed for clarity and peace in regard to loving my online "enemies," I thought about the critiques I've received. While the overwhelming majority of correspondence I get is encouraging and positive, there is still a fair amount of hate mail in my in-box and ugliness in certain comment sections across the blogosphere. While this is undoubtedly an expected consequence of writing and speaking publicly, especially on matters of heart, spirit, and soul, it can still sting. As much as I try to ignore the most vile of these messages, they can still be quite painful, and I think that's okay. As I said earlier, "Thick skin, tender heart"—and tenderheartedness can mean un-clenching my fists and letting some of these words hurt every now and again.

I mentioned on Facebook one day that an idea had popped into my mind: perhaps I could learn origami, that venerable Japanese paper craft, so that I might turn some of my hate mail into pretty birds and ships, flowers and kites. When I re-turned home from a trip to Kentucky, there was a box sitting by the front door: my friend Melissa, who is an artist, had sent me an origami kit.

I printed out some emails, I sat down at the dining-room table, and I began to fold—very slowly and clumsily at first. The best I could do at the beginning was a simple swan—but hey, this is the girl who was almost held back in kindergarten because of her regular outbursts during craft time, so I was pretty proud.

My fingers felt awkward. They weren't used to moving in these ways. They weren't accustomed to making creases and folding with precision. My eyes had to adjust as well, because they naturally gravitated to the painful words that I knew were on these pieces of paper. Forget about my heart; you know how I said this was a Lenten practice? It's called a prac-tice because it's an act of training, a discipline to do something you're not naturally inclined to do.

I followed the pattern in the book, folding these flat sheets of accusation into three-dimensional representations of something altogether different. Gradually, a wing emerged, and then another. Then a neck. Then a crooked little beak. Gradually, healing tears began to fall, and I let my fingers pray.

On and off for the next forty days, I let my fingers pray out more swans and then sailboats, flowers and then foxes. I learned some things: about reverse folds and crimp folds, about trial and error, about patience and perseverance, about retracing steps and following directions, about forgiveness and freedom, about redirecting some of my anxious, self-focused energy into purposeful acts of creativity and healing, about letting go and asking for help.

That last one—asking for help—might have been the most instructive lesson of all. Because sometimes you can't do it alone. I might imagine myself to be the consummate contemplative—call me Rachel of East Tennessee—but quiet meditation and poetic introspection are not my instinctive posture or my natural forte.

I remembered that my friend Melissa had mailed me the origami books.

I remembered that my brother-in-law, Tim, helped me fold my first sailboat.

I remembered that my friend Monika sat at my kitchen table with me. She took crayons and made blackout poems out of the most hateful letters—there isn't just one way to turn the ugly into the beautiful. And together we spent Holy Saturday forming crooked little pelicans, ducks, and penguins out of scraps of paper.

I remembered that a dear reader suggested I work some beautiful and affirming words into the process too. So I summoned the prayer of Teresa of Ávila and scribbled it onto a vibrant square of origami paper, and I wrote the fruits of the spirit onto another one.

I remembered that it was my sister, Amanda, who made a jumping frog while we waited to eat Easter dinner.

I remembered that it was Dan, my dear and skilled Dan, who crafted a perfect and precise crane in a few short minutes, while I managed to crumple up a yellow blob with only the vaguest resemblance to anything avian created by God.

I remembered that it was an author of one of those vile letters who, upon reading about my Lenten practice, took the time and energy to email me an apology—an origami bridge, I imagined, except in pixels, not paper. And it was that apology that inspired me to issue a few apologies of my own and to remind myself to be just a little quicker to listen, a little slower to speak, a little more restrained with any budding anger.

What I learned turning my hate mail into origami is that we are meant to remake this world together. We hurt together, and we are called to heal together, forgive together, and create together. And far from being all quiet and meditative and poetic and introspective, this practice turned out to be full of raucous laughter and cluttered tables, shared grumbles of frustration and chorused exclamations of delight.

Never has "That totally looks like a flamingo!" sounded so much like a hallelujah.

In a sense, even the people who continue to hate me and call me names—Jezebel, heretic, demon-possessed, satanic— were integral parts of this beautiful experience. Their words, carelessly spoken—or maybe carefully, because I haven't interviewed them about their thought, prayer, and writing processes—joined me in my home over those forty days, getting creased and folded, worked over and brushed aside to make room on the table for dinner, stepped on by a toddler and read aloud by my sister, stained with coffee and shoved haphazardly into the closet before guests arrived, blacked out and thrown away, turned into poems and transformed.

They have all helped me to remember that I am a very real human being, living a very real life, with a very real capacity to be hurt but also to be healed, to hate but also to love and be loved, to harm but also to forgive. So too with and for my enemies.

Something tells me that we might all be a bit more careful, a bit more gentle, if we knew how our words can travel through another's ear and linger for a long time in their soul. What if we imagined those words sitting on one another's kitchen tables, waiting to be reshaped? What if we knew just how much effort and time it might take to transform those ugly and heavy words into something beautiful and primed for flight, something that could float or fly away?

While I still haven't learned to fold any kind of origami tree, let alone a redwood, a swoop of cranes and a passel of pigeons occasionally regard me from my desk. They remind me of the power and potential we have together. You might not be able to hear the cranes' call or the pigeons' coo, but I can: They tell me that this world and this life are not mine alone. They whisper that we live in community, whether we like the other members or not. They teach me every time I look at them that belovedness belongs to us all.

# 14

# DWELLING IN SABBATH

wouldn't say that the evangelical culture of my childhood had a robust theology of rest or of Sabbath. I say it precisely that way because all Sabbath is rest, but not all rest is Sabbath.

When I was growing up, Sunday mornings were about Sunday school and then "grown-up" church. Not to name any names, but every member of the household who was a Held secretly harbored a hope of waking up with maybe just the slightest hint of a cold, because that would mean we could stay home—obviously, as an act of loving our fellow congregants—and watch Tim Russert on *Meet the Press* at 10 a.m.

My dad did have some vague Sabbath strictures: he didn't mow the lawn or do any yard work, and he made it a point for us to be together as a family on Sundays. Our meal routine hinted at Sabbath rest too, because my mom didn't want to cook on Sundays. When we lived in Alabama, we'd pick up some fried chicken and biscuits on the way home from church. After we moved to Dayton, we always went to Peking House, where the servers knew us well enough that we could just sit down and everyone else in the family would order "the usual"—cashew chicken for my dad, sesame chicken for my mom, and eight-treasure chicken for Amanda. True to form, I was the only nonconformist; sometimes I'd have a big bowl of wonton soup, other times the combination fried rice.

If it was football season, Sunday afternoons meant Dallas Cowboys games on the TV. (I grew up hearing stories of how my parents were in the stands for the legendary Thanksgiving 1974 Cowboys-Redskins game in which rookie backup QB Clint Longley, in for an injured Roger Staubach, hit Drew Pearson with a fifty-yard go-ahead TD pass with just seconds left on the clock.) And then everyone was also on their own for dinner. Sometimes Amanda and I would fry eggs or whip up a batch of pancakes. Other times, we'd pop some popcorn and follow that up with ice cream, and we'd call it good. Indeed, it was very good.

Our chef outfits were pretty unconventional. We always wore our best dresses to church every Sunday morning, and there's (probably more than) one family photo taken on a Sunday when I was wearing a particularly froufrou pink bow atop my head and some elaborate ruffles on the neckline of my white dress, as if I were a little porcelain Tudor princess doll. What Amanda and I loved most about dressing up was that, after church, Mom would let us just wear our lacy white slips—yes, we had to wear slips under those dresses, because we were *modest* and *proper young ladies*—around the house for the rest of the day, and we'd pretend we were fairy queens or brides. For all the questions I asked as an annoyingly curious kid, I never thought to wonder about the significance of a two-bride wedding.

As I've grown older, I've realized that the Sabbath has become a luxury product. It's most convenient for those whose lives are already marked by convenience, most accessible to those who have easy access to all that makes their lives easy.

It never occurred to me that my mom had the freedom not to cook because someone else was frying the chicken, baking the biscuits, or stir-frying the Chinese food. I've only recently understood that rest is not truly Sabbath if it depends on the labors of others who don't get to rest. Rest is not Sabbath if your comfort is contingent on others' discomfort. Rest is not Sabbath if it exacerbates inequity rather than diminishing it.

My point here isn't to shame us for our failures to keep the Sabbath. Because that too misunderstands what Sabbath is for, which is precisely the opposite of shame.

Much of the Book of Nehemiah is about building and rebuilding, doing and redoing. Nehemiah, a Jewish functionary in the court of the Assyrian King Artaxerxes, hears news about the sad state of Jerusalem. Early in the story, he gets permission from the king to go to the land of his ancestors to resurrect the holy city's walls and rebuild its gates. Most of the rest of the book is about not only physical renovation but also spiritual reconstruction. It's an Enneagram 3's dream, all that productivity.

Nehemiah emphasizes that the work of rebuilding Jerusalem is communal. He lists the names of various people who lead the effort as well as what gates and sections of the city walls they rebuilt. Tucked into this long list is a mention of a man named Shallum, who "made repairs, he and his daughters."[1] I love to imagine this band of sisters, hauling debris and laying brick and scraping mortar alongside the men under the blazing sun of a Jerusalem day.

Toward the end of the book, Nehemiah grieves deeply about the people's sin, and one of the main indictments is their disregard of the Sabbath. The workers are in the fields, the backs of the donkeys are laden with grain, and the marketplaces are bustling with shoppers. "What is this evil thing that you are doing, profaning the sabbath day?" Nehemiah says to the leaders.[2]

There are so many interesting details packed into just a few short verses: We see that foreigners are the chief salespeople, and the image of the burdened donkeys is particularly striking, in light of what the fourth commandment says about the day of rest: "Remember the sabbath day, and keep it holy. Six days you shall labor and do all your work. But the seventh day is a sabbath to the Lord your God; you shall not do any work—you, your son or your daughter, your male or female slave, your livestock, or the alien resident in your towns."[3]

The last part of that commandment is noteworthy: It names and acknowledges the social hierarchies of the time, flawed as they were. There are enslaved people. There are marginalized ones who somehow don't belong. And the call to rest is so sweeping that it even includes the cows and the donkeys, the sheep and the goats. Sabbath is for everyone and everything.

Nehemiah institutes Sabbath reforms. Just as the rebuilding effort was communal, so was the observance of the Sabbath: the very gates that had been rebuilt under Nehemiah's watch by the people of Jerusalem, men and women, were guarded so that the holy day of rest might be kept and honored by all. This was not a matter of mere legalism, and the way that passage ends is especially moving: it invokes the majesty of God's steadfast love.

What God's love—and our belovedness—has to do with the Sabbath command might seem opaque. But in his book *Wrestling with Rest*, the practical theologian Nathan T. Stucky, citing Karl Barth, points out something I had never before noticed: Sabbath rest is not a reward that God gave humanity for a productive week. The very first Sabbath day was also humans' very first full day of existence. In other words, they hadn't done a thing. "That's why human participation in Sabbath rest on the seventh day of creation couldn't be based in human accomplishment. It could be grounded only in God's work and invitation," Stucky writes. "The only work that humans have to reflect on at this point is God's. . . . From the beginning, then, God gives Sabbath rest as a gift of sheer grace."[4]

Sabbath rest was never meant to be our end. Instead, it was and is our beginning, infused with God's steadfast love as expressed through God's grace of time to enjoy and soak in God's creativity.

Years ago, my dear friend Sarah Bessey wrote an essay about Sabbath that slapped me in the face. "You can go go go go go go and you can do do do do do and you can tell yourself things like 'Good things come to those who hustle' and you can pride yourself on your work ethic," she wrote. "It's permissible. (But it is not beneficial.)"[5] The reality is that we weren't created to go go go or to do do do. We were made to be. And so Sarah summoned us to remember that, starting with just one day— one day of rest, one day of renewal, one day of respite from the incessant demands of work and life.

"Start with the one day, this week," Sarah wrote, "and declare a slender victory for the gift of being human in God's good and gorgeous world, created with pleasure and delight."[6]

The key words there, I think, are "the gift of being human in God's good and gorgeous world." In that phrase, we are reminded of who we are in the context of who God is in the context of what God has done. We are creatures. We are created beings. And it is the Creator, and the heart behind the creation, that the Sabbath reminds us of.

When Jesus healed on the Sabbath, his legalistic critics and opponents were infuriated. But what he was doing was entirely in keeping with the point of the Sabbath, which was to honor the beauty, dignity, and integrity of what God had made. What he was doing was in fact an *undoing*—undoing the dishonor that some humans had heaped upon other humans, undoing the disregard of our equal standing before

God as God's creation, undoing the harm and the marginalization that had occurred when some humans centered themselves and their manmade hierarchies.

I think of all those who were healed on the Sabbath—and let me be clear about how I see these healings: I don't think Jesus regarded any of those he healed as less than because of their disabilities. Rather, he acknowledged that *society* saw them as such. When he healed a woman who, according to the Gospel of Luke, had been bent under the weight of an evil spirit for eighteen years, he named her as a "daughter of Abraham"—an honorific that underlined her intrinsic worth.[7] When he was on his way to a senior Pharisee's house for a Shabbat meal and cured a man with dropsy (edema) en route, he followed it up with a dinnertime teaching about hospitality and welcome and honoring those who have been dishonored.[8]

If the Sabbath is about wholeness and about being the people God created us to be, equal and loved, thriving and flourishing, could there be anything more right than for him to heal on that holy day? And if the Sabbath is about wholeness and about the people whom God created us to be, equal and loved, thriving and flourishing, could there be anything more right than for us to turn wholeheartedly toward our own healing on that holy day?

There might have been moments as you've read these pages when you've felt frustration and even despair, because it has seemed as if I am asking you to do more, try something different, think in a way you've never thought before. So many instructions! So many demands!

My point in dwelling on the Sabbath—my own hope in dwelling *in* Sabbath—is to remember that our beginnings were grace and rest, and our ends will be too. If there's any truth in any of this Christianity thing, it is that our existence started with rest, with the opportunity to glory in having earned nothing and done nothing, and it will find its culmination in rest, with the joy of feasting in the knowledge that we earned none of this abundance and had to do nothing to enjoy this goodness, nothing, that is, other than to simply receive.

I wonder if God instituted the rhythm of Sabbath because, in God's infinite wisdom, there was a deep recognition that we'd need to try and try again even to begin to comprehend this truth. We'd need another week of practice. We'd need another six days of chasing love and proving ourselves before we ended up exhausted and spent, ready to surrender to rest. We'd need a reminder of grace, and then another, and then another.

It goes against everything in me to accept that God would ask us to do *less*, not more. But then I think of the liberated delight of a younger me, the one who reveled in a multicourse meal of popcorn and ice cream for Sunday dinner, shared with my beloved little sister, and it begins to make more sense. I felt . . . free. I can name that now. And somehow, in that freedom, I could just be.

I don't know what might be on your version of that Sunday-dinner menu. I don't know who might—or might not—be in the room, so that you can laugh or cry or mope or scream or play as you need to. I don't know what it might take so that your questions would be cast aside, so that your worries and concerns might settle down momentarily, so that your fists might unclench and you might catch your breath and your soul might unfold, just a little bit, to what God has for you.

Unfold to rest.

Unfold to Sabbath.

Unfold to grace.

Unfold to love.

# EPILOGUE

# TELOS

Dan and I have bought a piece of land just a few minutes' drive from our current house. We're building a new house there.

In that house, as in the one we occupy now, my desk will be in the basement. But this basement will be different. There won't be any of that 1970s wood paneling or fraying carpet. There will be wide windows. There will be abundant light.

In my mind's eye, I'm already sitting at my desk in that basement, tapping away at my keyboard and trying (and failing) to stay off Twitter. I'm watching my kids play in the grass outside, their little blond heads framed by the broad sky and the tall trees in the distance. I'm seeing the birds bear witness from above, zipping back and forth to tend to their own young, in their own nests, somewhere in the nearby woods. I'm imagining that we'll all be doing what we were meant to do.

My hope is that our new house will be a house built on love. That as my son and daughter play, they'll know how much their parents love them. That as they pluck a weed and declare it a flower, as they jump into piles of autumn leaves and then watch as the trees turn lush, full, and green again, as they turn toward the sun and delight in its warmth, they'll know how much their God loves them, and that out of all that love, they in turn will learn how to love too.

So we have come to the end. But as Scripture reminds us, the end is never quite the end as we typically understand it; it's only a beginning.

One of the biblical words for "end" is *telos*. This Greek word doesn't have the air of finality that the English word "end" has. In other words, it's not a dead end. To the contrary, it's full of life, because it has a sense of completion and contentment. It carries the satisfaction of doing what you know you're called to do and the fulfillment of being who you were always meant to be.

The telos of an apple tree is to flower and to fruit, producing blossoms and apples and seeds that will propagate the next generation of tree.

The telos of a honeybee is to collect pollen and produce honey, working in concert with other honeybees throughout seasons of plenty to store sustenance for seasons of lack.

The telos of a surfboard is to help the surfer catch a wave.

The telos of wine and bread is to sustain and to nourish, to delight the taste buds and to gratify the body until the next meal comes.

The telos of the Alabama Crimson Tide football program is to produce national championships and remind Auburn of their proper, lower place in the divinely blessed order of things.

The telos of a human—your telos, my telos, our telos—is to love lavishly and indiscriminately, as our God has loved us. Love is what we were made to do. But even more than that, love is who we were made to be.

One of the first Bible verses that a kid typically learns is John 3:16. It's taken me some time to come to this conclusion, but maybe it's not such a bad place for us to end: "For God so loved the world . . ."

> For God so loved the world that God made us for love.
> For God so loved the world that God incarnated love
>     itself in the person of Jesus.
> For God so loved the world that God empowered us
>     to love even our enemies, even the worst person
>     on Twitter, even those who seem incapable of love
>     themselves.
> For God so loved the world that God called us to
>     death—indeed walked ahead of us to death—
>     because God knew that, on the other side, we'd
>     find resurrection.

Despite what the world might have you believe, love isn't weak. Love has the toughness to endure even amidst the worst of humanity. Love has the strength to survive even the ugliest of bigotry, even the most murderous hatreds. Love has the resilience to rise again, even when the world has declared it dead. And this love is what you and I were made for, even if it seems so very far away.

"To measure the full distance between where we are and where God created us to be—to suffer that distance, to name it, to decide not to live quietly with it any longer," Barbara Brown Taylor writes, "that is the moment when we know we are dead and begin to decide who we will be tomorrow."[1] If your telos, my telos, and our telos is to love, you know as well as I do how impossible this seems and how impossible this is. We can't do it in and of ourselves. And we can't do it if we don't feel loved ourselves.

It can be difficult for those of us living in a culture that prizes earning power above nearly everything else to understand that in the economy of grace, the currency of deserved and undeserved is irrelevant. It is absolutely true that you can't earn God's love. But it's not because you are a helpless wretch whose sin makes it impossible for God to even look at you or because you have done something so grievously wrong that your soul has been permanently stained, as if by spiritual Sharpie. The truth is, you can't earn God's love because you already have it. You can't be any more loved than you are because God's love has already been freely and abundantly given. You can't do anything to achieve a greater portion of God's love because God's love for you is already unconditional and it is already infinite.

If you're anything like I am, the stories I've told and the observations I've shared might have worn away some of your doubt, but ever so slowly, like water gently and gradually weathering away the rock. My hope has been to hint at your *telos*, but I'm pretty sure that even with my stunning array of Best Christian Attitude Awards, I don't have the power to deliver you to it.

In John 13, the Beloved Apostle writes that "Jesus knew that his hour had come to depart from this world." It's a remarkable thing to reflect on this story: the One who embodied love also broke bread with his friends, and laughed with them, and delighted in them, and wept with them, and shared their burdens. "Having loved his own who were in the world," John wrote, "he loved them to the end."[2]

You could, of course, read this literally: he loved them to the end of his life on Earth. But "end" here—*telos*, in the original Greek—means more than that, because Jesus and his love were more than that. He loved them to perfection. He loved them with a boundless love that surpassed anything ever experienced in this life. He loved them to the fullness of who they were and whom they could become.

The *telos* of a human—your *telos*, my *telos*, our *telos*—is to love lavishly and indiscriminately *because we have been loved lavishly and indiscriminately.* We can be gracious because we are grateful. We can love because we have been loved.

On the days when I believe, I know all this to be true. On the days when you believe, I hope you'll know this to be true too. I hope you'll feel deep within your heart and with every cell of your being that you are held and embraced by the God who made you, the God who redeemed you, and the God who accompanies you through every end and onward to every beginning.

Even on the days when I'm not sure I can believe it wholeheartedly, this is still the story I'm willing to be wrong about.

Amen.

# AFTERWORD

My tattoo artist doesn't ask me the question I wish he would. It's May 2019 and I am sitting in his chair, worn and familiar, while he takes a disposable razor and removes the fine hair on my forearm. I'd been here many times before, usually relaxed and chatty, but now I'm shifting awkwardly, like an amateur. I am quietly trudging through the deep grief of losing my friend. He doesn't ask what the odd words mean that he is applying to my skin, *eshet chayil*—a memorial tattoo for Rachel Held Evans.

Over the last six years, Rachel and I had stood onstage together many times—her, a short, pretty, Southern young woman in a cardigan, and me, a tall, tattooed city gal in jeans and a black tank top. Rachel always delighted in telling the audience, "I'm so glad Nadia and I became friends as adults because if we had known each other in high school, she would have just scared the bejeezus out of me."

We didn't look like we would be friends. If we had met as eleven-year-olds, though, I promise that we would have been more like a matched set: walking into church in our Sunday school shoes, carrying our well-highlighted NIV Bibles, soaking up everything we were taught about how to be "good girls." Rachel and I were church kids. Faith was our first language.

Then at some point our faith unraveled. We began to question what we were taught to accept. But here is where my path and Rachel's diverged. When Rachel began to doubt, when she tilted her head to one side and looked at the church and the Bible and doctrine from a different angle, she didn't just get angry, say f*ck it, walk away, and consume all the drugs and alcohol she could get her hands on, like I did. Rachel got to *work*. While I settled for rebelling against Christianity, she strove to redeem it. She studied Scripture and the history of interpretation. She wasn't afraid of hard questions. She pointed out when the teachings of the church were nothing more than camouflage for bias. When others could see only the letter of faith, she insisted on the *spirit* of it. And perhaps there is no better example of Rachel at her finest than her work on what many women in the church have been told is "The Proverbs 31 woman."

There are twenty-two lines of poetry in the 31st chapter of Proverbs, which begin, "Who can find a virtuous woman?" or, with the original Hebrew, "Who can find an *eshet chayil?*" The verses that follow describe the actions of an upper-class wife: she wakes while it's still night and makes her husband food; she sews and buys and mends and plants and manages their household-based business. The intention of these verses is to model for a husband how to notice and then praise the work and accomplishments of his wife. And yet an entire evangelical industry has popped up around it, urging women to attain the cherished status as a "Proverbs 31 wife." Rachel wrote in *A Year of Biblical Womanhood*, her genius book about trying to live for a year according to every biblical rule for women,

"No longer presented as a song through which a man offers his wife praise, Proverbs 31 is presented as a task list through which the woman earns it. . . . We turned an anthem into an assignment."[1]

The best translation of *eshet chayil* is not "woman of virtue" but actually "woman of *valor*," and as Rachel taught us, the most faithful use of Proverbs 31 is not as an unattainable standard women must reach in order to be worthy of praise but as an example of how much in women's lives and work is *already* worthy of praise.

For years, when one of her friends had a baby, finally went into therapy, got a new job, published a book, successfully ordered a pizza to feed her family, confronted injustice, finished a bachelor's degree in her sixties, or just remembered to pick up the dry cleaning, Rachel exclaimed, "Woman of valor!" Because, she reminded us, there is valor—bravery, courage, and strength—in our actions as women.

Rachel turned an assignment into an anthem.

My tattoo artist isn't asking about any of this, of course, but I'm thinking about every single bit of it while I silently, prayerfully, have *eshet chayil* tattooed on my arm.

Because twenty-six days before sitting in a tattoo chair I had stood in an ICU room at a Nashville hospital with a small circle of her family and friends. We surrounded her bed to say goodbye as she passed from this life to the next. We prayed and cried and sang and anointed her and struggled to understand why this was happening, why a woman so young, with so much more to write, with so many more years to live with her beloved, with so many more days to raise and cherish her babies, with so many more adventures to take on with her friends, was minutes away from dying. (My friend Rachel did not settle for platitudes or easy answers and so neither will I offer any here.)

I paused to look at a collage of pictures taped to her hospital room wall, including one of her holding a homemade sign that read, "Dan is awesome!" She was standing next to the WELCOME TO DAYTON sign in her beloved hometown in Tennessee, an act she had done in honor of Proverbs 31:23, "Her husband is respected at the city gates." I smiled at the grace and good humor Rachel had always applied to her life and her work, grateful for the too-brief gift of it.

Below the pictures sat a small table on which Dan, Rachel's husband, had affectionately displayed a stack of her books and beside which he had written a note to the hospital staff: "Rachel is my wife, mother to my children, and best friend. She is also an accomplished writer. Her generous spirit is an inspiration. Her work impacted thousands. Her life was a gift to us all."

PROVERBS 31:28–29
Her husband . . . praises her:
"Many women have done excellently,
but you surpass them all."

RACHEL HELD EVANS

*June 8, 1981–May 4, 2019*

Rachel was a Woman of Valor to the very end. When we said goodbye to her a month later, at her funeral in Chattanooga,

I offered a version of the benediction I first published in my book *Accidental Saints*, which names all the kinds of people both Rachel and Jesus loved so well. But I ended the blessing with a passage from Rachel's own book *Inspired*. Because she did always love having the last word. As well she should.

> Blessed are the agnostics.
> Blessed are they who doubt.
> Blessed are those who have nothing to offer.
> Blessed are the preschoolers who cut in line at
> communion.
> Blessed are the poor in spirit.
> You are of heaven and Jesus blesses you.
> Blessed are those whom no one else notices. The
> kids who sit alone at middle school lunch tables. The
> laundry guys at the hospital. The sex workers and
> the night-shift street sweepers. The closeted. The teens
> who have to figure out ways to hide the new cuts on
> their arms.
> Blessed are the meek.
> You are of heaven and Jesus blesses you.
> Blessed are they who have loved enough to know
> what loss feels like.
> Blessed are the mothers of the miscarried. Blessed
> are they who can't fall apart because they have to keep
> it together for everyone else. Blessed are those who "still
> aren't over it yet."
> Blessed are those who mourn.
> You are of heaven and Jesus blesses you.

I imagine Jesus standing here blessing us because that is our Lord's nature. This Jesus cried at his friend's tomb, turned the other cheek, and forgave those who hung him on a cross. He was God's Beatitude—God's blessing to the weak in a world that admires only the strong.

Jesus invites us into a story bigger than ourselves and our imaginations, yet we all get to tell that story with the scandalous particularity of this moment and this place. We are storytelling creatures because we are fashioned in the image of a storytelling God. May we never neglect that gift. May we never lose our love for telling the story.

Amen.

—the Rev. Nadia Bolz-Weber

# NOTES

*Prologue: Because They Said Yes*

1. Jer. 29:11 (NIV).
2. Gen. 16:13 (NRSV). In *Womanist Midrash*, the Rev. Dr. Wilda Gafney translates it "God of seeing" ([Louisville, KY: Westminster John Knox, 2017], 43), whereas Robert Alter writes in his translation of the Hebrew Bible that "the most evident meaning of the Hebrew name would be 'God Who sees me'" (*The Five Books of Moses* [New York: W. W. Norton, 2004], 80).
3. Mark 16:3 (NRSV).
4. Matt. 28:1–8; Mark 16:1–8; Luke 23:55–24:11; John 20:1-2.
5. John 20:18; Matt. 28:7 (NRSV).
6. Nadia Bolz-Weber, *Pastrix: The Cranky Beautiful Faith of a Sinner and Saint* (New York: Jericho Books, 2013), 138.
7. Madeleine L'Engle, *And It Was Good: Reflections on Beginnings*, (New York: Crown, 2017), 15.
8. L'Engle, *And It Was Good*, 15.

*Chapter 1: On the Days When I Believe*

1. Deut. 6:4–5 (NIV).
2. Deut. 6:7 (NRSV).
3. Matt. 22:37–39 (NRSV).
4. Heb. 11:1 (NRSV).
5. Ann Patchett, *Commonwealth* (New York: Harper Perennial, 2020), 258.

# NOTES

*Chapter 2: My Wicked Little Heart*

1. DC Talk, "Jesus Freak," by Mark Heimermann and Toby McKeehan, track 3 on *Jesus Freak*, Forefront Communications, 1995.
2. Ernest Kurtz and Katherine Ketcham, *The Spirituality of Imperfection: Storytelling and the Search for Meaning* (New York: Bantam, 1992), 2.
3. 1 Cor. 2:11b (NRSV).
4. 1 Cor. 13:12 (NRSV).
5. Thomas Merton, *No Man Is an Island* (Boulder, CO: Shambhala, 2005), 245.
6. Anne Lamott, *Plan B: Further Thoughts on Faith* (New York: Riverhead, 2006), 257.

*Chapter 3: Where Stone Becomes Flesh*

1. Ezek. 36:26 (NRSV).
2. Global Oneness Project, "Turning to Face the Dark: A Conversation Between Rabbi Dr. Ariel Burger and Parker Palmer," interview, May 2019, https://www.globalonenessproject.org/library/interviews/turning-face-dark?fbclid=IwAR08M5GGTySOlEvEq727fgbElCi-vgl2dcG69g37w_cypiefBGPJ4Auf3n8.
3. Brené Brown, *The Gifts of Imperfection: Let Go of Who You Think You're Supposed to Be and Embrace Who You Are* (Center City, MN: Hazelden, 2010), 1.
4. Brown, *The Gifts of Imperfection*, 21.
5. Ps. 10:1 (NRSV).
6. Eccles. 1:14 (NRSV).
7. Daniel Trotta, "Letters Reveal Mother Teresa's Doubt About Faith," Reuters, August 24, 2007, https://in.reuters.com/article/idINIndia-29140020070824.
8. Daniel Taylor, *The Myth of Certainty: The Reflective Christian and the Risk of Commitment* (Downers Grove, IL: InterVarsity, 1992), 97.
9. Justo L. Gonzalez, *The Apostles' Creed for Today* (Louisville, KY: Westminster John Knox, 2007), 8.
10. Gonzalez, *The Apostles' Creed for Today*, 9.

## Chapter 4: The Liberation of the Know-It-All

1. 1 Pet. 3:15 (NRSV).
2. 1 Pet. 3:15; 1 Pet. 3:13 (NRSV).
3. Deut. 6:4–5 (NRSV).
4. Matt. 14:31 (NRSV).
5. 1 Pet. 4:8 (NRSV).
6. Rachel Musleah, "Profile: Angela Buchdahl," *Hadassah Magazine*, June/July 2013, https://www.hadassahmagazine.org/2013/06/26 /profile-angela-buchdahl/.
7. Miguel de Unamuno, *The Tragic Sense of Life*, trans. J. E. Crawford Flitch (New York: Dover, 1954), https://www.gutenberg.org/files /14636/14636-h/14636-h.htm.

## Chapter 5: Thick Skin, Tender Heart

1. Lois Tverberg, *Walking in the Dust of Rabbi Jesus: How the Jewish Words of Jesus Can Change Your Life* (Grand Rapids, MI: Zondervan, 2013), 46.
2. Amy-Jill Levine and Marc Zvi Brettler, eds., *The Jewish Annotated New Testament* (New York: Oxford Univ. Press, 2011), 10.
3. Jonathan Haidt, *The Righteous Mind: Why Good People Are Divided by Politics and Religion* (New York: Vintage, 2013), 32–34.
4. Plato, *Timaeus* 42, trans. Benjamin Jowett (New York: Random House, 1937), 23.
5. Tverberg, *Walking in the Dust of Rabbi Jesus*, 38.
6. "Devarim—Deuteronomy—Chapter 6," verse 5, *Tanakh—The Hebrew Bible*, Chabad.org, https://www.chabad.org/library/bible_cdo/aid/9970 /showrashi/true/jewish/Chapter-6.htm#lt=primary.
7. "What Is the Shema? Intro to the Most Important Jewish Prayer," posted by BimBam, October 11, 2018, video, 3:25, https://www.youtube .com/watch?v=9geXjErjvfw.

## Chapter 6: Jonathan Edwards Is Not My Homeboy

1. Keen-eyed readers with sharp memories might recall seeing a different first name in the 2013 blog post. When they shared their story on the

blog, Eve Ettinger, who uses the pronouns they/them, was known as Hännah Ettinger.

2. C. J. Mahaney, "Better Than I Deserve—Philippians 2:14–18," from the series *Pressing on in Joy (The Book of Philippians)*, January 13, 2013, audio recording, 48:30, https://www.sgclouisville.org/mediaPlayer/# /sermonaudio/19.

3. Hännah Ettinger, "Growing Up in SGM," *Rachel Held Evans* (blog), June 27, 2013, https://rachelheldevans.com/blog/growing-up-in -sovereign-grace-ministries-abuse.

4. Ettinger, "Growing Up in SGM."

5. Book of Concord, "The Formula of Concord: Solid Declaration," section I, article 11, https://bookofconcord.org/formula-of-concord -solid-declaration/article-xi/.

6. Jonathan Edwards, "Sinners in the Hands of an Angry God (Enfield, CT, 1741)," in *Sinners in the Hands of an Angry God and Other Puritan Sermons* (Mineola, NY: Dover, 2005), 178.

7. Thomas Hardy, *Tess of the d'Urbervilles: A Pure Woman* (Minneapolis: Lerner, 2014), 34.

8. Collin Hansen, "Young, Restless, Reformed," *Christianity Today*, September 22, 2006, https://www.christianitytoday.com/ct/2006 /september/42.32.html.

9. This is as good a place as any to note the distinction between the New Calvinism movement I encountered in college and the broader tradition of Calvinism and Reformed theology of which there are many variations, including more progressive ones.

10. John Piper, "Tsunami and Repentance," *Desiring God* (blog), January 5, 2005, https://www.desiringgod.org/articles/tsunami -and-repentance.

11. Daniel James Ladinsky, "God Would Kneel Down," from *Love Poems from God: Twelve Sacred Voices from the East and West* (New York: Penguin Compass, 2002); used with permission.

12. Zeph. 3:17; Isa. 43:1; Jer. 31:3 (NRSV).

13. Rom. 8:38–39 (NRSV).

14. Brown, *The Gifts of Imperfection*, 26.

15. Brené Brown, *Daring Greatly: How the Courage to Be Vulnerable*

NOTES

*Transforms the Way We Live, Love, Parent, and Lead* (New York:
Penguin Random House, 2015), 145.
16. Brown, *Daring Greatly*, 9.

## Chapter 7: Beginning Again with Love

1. Danielle Shroyer, *Original Blessing: Putting Sin in Its Rightful Place*
(Minneapolis: Fortress, 2016), xi.
2. Gen. 3:8 (NRSV).
3. Prov. 3:18 (NRSV).
4. Prov. 8:35–36 (NRSV).
5. Prov. 9:10; Eccles. 1:14 (NRSV). Here, though I quote the familiar,
traditional English translation, I am also wary of it. Note that Rabbi
Abraham Joshua Heschel preferred to translate the Hebrew *yirah* as
"awe," which does not carry the negative, danger-invoking connotations
of the English word "fear."
6. Carlos Mesters, *Eden: Golden Age or Goad to Action?* (Maryknoll, NY:
Orbis, 1974), 52.
7. Gen. 3:7 (NRSV).
8. Shroyer, *Original Blessing*, 32.
9. Lisa Sharon Harper, *The Very Good Gospel: How Everything Wrong
Can Be Made Right* (Colorado Springs, CO: WaterBrook, 2016),
32–33, 50.
10. 1 John 4:7–8 (NRSV).
11. 1 John 4:16b (NRSV).

## Chapter 8: From Death to Life

1. Don Richard Riso and Russ Hudson, *The Wisdom of the Enneagram:
The Complete Guide to Psychological and Spiritual Growth for the Nine
Personality Types* (New York: Bantam, 1999), 153–55.
2. Mark 8:33 (NRSV).
3. Burton L. Visotzky, *Reading the Book: Making the Bible a Timeless Text*
(New York: Jewish Publication Society, 2010), 10.

4. Visotzky, *Reading the Book*, 12.

5. Leonard Sweet, *The Well-Played Life: Why Pleasing God Doesn't Have to Be Such Hard Work* (Carol Stream, IL: Tyndale House, 2014), 102.

6. Sweet, *The Well-Played Life*, 102.

7. Rom. 8:21 (NRSV).

## Chapter 9: The Steady Work of Living Water

1. Mark 1:11 (NRSV).

2. Amy-Jill Levine, *Short Stories by Jesus: The Enigmatic Parables of a Controversial Rabbi* (New York: HarperOne, 2015), 14.

3. Acts 10:34–35 (NIV).

4. Acts 10:28 (NIV).

## Chapter 10: Many Voices, Many Masks

1. John 6:7 (NRSV).

2. Gen. 30:1 (NRSV).

3. Wilda C. Gafney, *Womanist Midrash: A Reintroduction to the Women of the Torah and the Throne* (Louisville, KY: Westminster John Knox, 2017), 62.

4. Gen. 35:18 (NRSV).

5. Susan Niditch, "Genesis," in *Women's Bible Commentary*, eds. Carol A. Newsom, Sharon H. Ringe, and Jacqueline E. Lapsley (Louisville, KY: Westminster John Knox, 2012), 40.

6. Henri J. M. Nouwen, *Life of the Beloved* (Chestnut Ridge, NY: Crossroad, 2002), 153.

## Chapter 11: Wilderness

1. Delores S. Williams, *Sisters in the Wilderness: The Challenge of Womanist God-Talk* (Maryknoll, NY: Orbis, 1993), 19.

2. Gen. 16:11 (NRSV).

3. Gen. 21:11–12 (NRSV).

4. Gen. 21:17 (NRSV).

5. Williams, *Sisters in the Wilderness*, 32.

6. Gen. 21:20 (NRSV).

# NOTES

7. Kaitlin B. Curtice, *Glory Happening: Finding the Divine in Everyday Places* (Brewster, MA: Paraclete, 2017), 6.
8. Curtice, *Glory Happening*, 6-7.
9. Deut. 1:31 (NRSV).

## Chapter 12: God Has Made a Home with Us

1. Madeleine L'Engle, *The Genesis Trilogy* (Colorado Springs, CO: WaterBrook, 2001), 222.
2. L'Engle, *The Genesis Trilogy*, 222.
3. L'Engle, *The Genesis Trilogy*, 222.
4. Ellen F. Davis, *Getting Involved with God: Rediscovering the Old Testament* (Lanham, MD: Rowman & Littlefield, 2001), 8.
5. Ps. 44:8, 9, 23 (NRSV).
6. Ps. 58:8 (NRSV).
7. Ps. 88:6, 8 (NRSV).
8. Davis, *Getting Involved with God*, 8.
9. Luke 1:47–55 (NRSV).
10. Frederick Buechner, *Whistling in the Dark: An ABC Theologized* (New York: Harper & Row, 1988), 43.
11. Buechner, *Whistling in the Dark*, 43.
12. Davis, *Getting Involved with God*, 11.
13. Ps. 102:9–11 (NRSV).
14. Davis, *Getting Involved with God*, 163.
15. Ps. 102:17 (NRSV).
16. Davis, *Getting Involved with God*, 12.

## Chapter 13: Loving Our Enemies

1. Job 14:7–9 (NRSV).
2. Simone Weil, *The Need for Roots: Prelude to a Declaration of Duties Towards Mankind* (New York: Routledge, 2002), 41.
3. Visotzky, *Reading the Book*, 4.
4. James H. Cone, *God of the Oppressed* (Maryknoll, NY: Orbis, 2018).
5. Jon Ward, "Huckabee's 'Welcome to Hell' Stands Out from GOP Bin Laden Responses Downplaying Obama," *HuffPost*, May 2,

2011, https://www.huffpost.com/entry/huckabees-welcome-to
-hell_n_856186.

6. Rachel Held Evans, "What Our Enemy Brought Out in Us . . ."
*Rachel Held Evans* (blog), May 2, 2011, https://rachelheldevans.com
/blog/osama-bin-laden-death-christians.

7. Evolving Faith, "The Evolving Faith Podcast, Season 1 Episode 12:
Enemies, Empathy, and Shalom with Osheta Moore," transcript,
September 9, 2020, https://evolvingfaith.com/all-podcast-episodes
/ep-12-osheta-moore.

8. David Zaslow, "The Deeper Meaning of Shalom," RabiDavidZaslow
.com, January 5, 2004, https://rabbidavidzaslow.com/the-deeper
-meaning-of-shalom/.

9. Isa. 2:4 (NRSV).

## Chapter 14: Dwelling in Sabbath

1. Neh. 3:12 (NRSV).
2. Neh. 13:17 (NRSV).
3. Exod. 20:8–10 (NRSV).
4. Nathan T. Stucky, *Wrestling with Rest: Inviting Youth to Discover the Gift of Sabbath* (Grand Rapids, MI: William B. Eerdmans, 2019), 107.
5. Sarah Bessey, "Start Small, Start with Sabbath," SheLovesMagazine
.com, August 18, 2012, https://shelovesmagazine.com/2012/start
-small/.
6. Bessey, "Start Small, Start with Sabbath."
7. Luke 13:16 (NRSV).
8. Luke 14:1–11 (NRSV).

## Epilogue: Telos

1. Barbara Brown Taylor, *Speaking of Sin: The Lost Language of Salvation* (London, UK: Canterbury, 2015), 43.
2. John 13:1 (NRSV).

## Afterword

1. Rachel Held Evans, *A Year of Biblical Womanhood: How a Liberated Woman Found Herself* (Nashville: Thomas Nelson, 2012), 76, 89.

# ABOUT THE AUTHORS

**Rachel Held Evans** (1981–2019) was the *New York Times* bestselling author of *Inspired, Searching for Sunday, A Year of Biblical Womanhood, Faith Unraveled*, and *What Is God Like?* (with Matthew Paul Turner and illustrated by Ying Hui Tan). Rachel's words about faith, doubt, and life were featured not only on her own blog but also in numerous publications, including *The Washington Post, The Guardian*, and *The Huffington Post.* She appeared on NPR, BBC, *The Today Show*, and *The View*, and served on President Obama's Advisory Council on Faith-based and Neighborhood Partnerships. She lived with her husband and two children in Dayton, Tennessee.

**Jeff Chu** is cocurator of the Evolving Faith conference, alongside Sarah Bessey, who founded the gathering with Rachel Held Evans. He is also the author of *Does Jesus Really Love Me?* and an editor-at-large at *Travel + Leisure*. He, his husband, Tristan, and their dog, Fozzie, make their home in Grand Rapids, Michigan.